KNOWLEDGE MANAGEMENT AND INFORMATION TECHNOLOGY

KNOWLEDGE MANAGEMENT AND INFORMATION TECHNOLOGY

C.S.R. Prabhu

GYAN

ISBN: 978-81-212-1219-9

Price: ₹ 570

First Published 2014

Published by

Gyan Publishing House
23, Main Ansari Road, Daryaganj,
New Delhi - 110002
Phones : 23282060, 23261060
Fax : (011) 23285914
E-mail: books@gyanbooks.com
website: gyanbooks.com

Laser Typesetting: Rajender Vashist, Delhi
Printed at: G. Print Process, Delhi

Cataloging in Publication Data--DK
Courtesy: D.K. Agencies (P) Ltd. <docinfo@dkagencies.com>

Prabhu, C. S. R.
Knowledge management and IT / C.S.R. Prabhu.
p. cm.
Includes bibliographical references.
ISBN 9788121212199

1. Knowledge management. 2. Organizational learning. 3. Information technology. I. Title. II. Title: Knowledge management and information technology.

DDC 658.4038 23

Contents

Preface

Organisational knowledge and its management is critical to an organisation. A learning organisation implements the organisational Knowledge Management in such a way that all the employees are kept upto date and adequately competent in their professional knowledge and skills so that they can perform their regular duties, upto the mark of expectation, thereby keeping the organisation competent and competitive. Learning organisations which are also usually teaching organisations, will not only survive in competitive environment but also excel in their own professional areas of specialisation to the highest level. Due to rapid changes in Information Technology (IT) all IT organisations have no choice but to be competent and competitive in their respective areas of work. Also, a competent IT organisation has to be definitely a learning organisation, ensuring meaningful knowledge upgradation and knowledge management, including knowledge transfer.

In this book the importance of Knowledge Management is brought out for Information Technology Organisations.

Different schools of approaches to Knowledge Management are presented and compared with each other.

All the three phases of Knowledge Management life cycle : Map, Build and Operationalise, are covered.

Critical Success Factors, Enablers for Knowledge Management (KM) alongwith Knowledge Transfer (KT) are covered. Advancede topics as Distributed Knowledge Management System (DKMS), Object Knowledge Model (OKM) are also covered.

The book has KM Case Studies from leading IT organisations as Infosys and other telecom organisations as Samsung, Airtel and also representative companies from other sectors such as CITE, Unilever, Goldsun, Bank of Indonesia, etc., to give glimpses of Knowledge Management implementation in a wide spectrum of domains.

C.S.R. Prabhu

Acknowledgements

I acknowledge with thanks the assistance provided by Shri Girish of National Productive Council, Chennai, Shri B.M. Rao and Shri H.S. Venkateshwara of National Informatics Centre, Hydereabad.

C.S.R. Prabhu

1

Knowledge and its Management in an Organisation

In any organisational environment, the strategic and vitally fundamental components are its data, information and knowledge.

Data is defined as any manifestation in the environment which may include symbolic representations that, in combination, may form the basis of information.

Information is defined as data in context, to which meaning has been attributed.

Knowledge is defined as a body of understanding and skills of people, increased by interaction with others and with information which may be made available through a variety of sources such as books, magazines, databases, Internet, etc.

Knowledge has many facets:

- Personal and sub-consciously understood knowledge, residing within the person's mind including abstract aspects such as Culture or other forms of "tacit knowledge".
- Documented structured or unstructured knowledge such as documents, images, films or any other multimedia forms of knowledge.

- The organisational knowledge asset base.

Knowledge Enablers are those specific tools or processes or methodologies which help in management of knowledge.

1.1. Knowledge Management (KM)

Knowledge Management (KM) is the activity of managing organisational knowledge.

Knowledge Management (KM) is an interdisciplinary approach for improving organisational outputs, outcomes and organisational learning through the maximisation of the use of knowledge by all concerned in the organisation. KM includes the design, implementation and review of all activities and processes in the organisation; to improve the processes of creation, sharing and application of knowledge in the organisation.

KM has been variously defined:

- KM refers to policies, procedures and technologies employed for operating a continuously updated linked pair of networked databases.[1]
- KM refers to the processes of capturing, distributing and effectively using knowledge.[2]
- KM is the capability of a company to create new knowledge, disseminate it throughout the organisation and embody it in products, services and systems.[3]
- KM is a systematic approach to find, understand and use knowledge to create value.[4]
- KM caters to the critical issues of organisational adoption, survival and competence in the face of increasingly discontinuous environmental change. Essentially, it embodies organisational processes that seek synergistic combination of the data and information processing capacity of information

technologies and the creative and innovative capacity of human beings.[5], and

- KM is the process of increasing the efficiency of knowledge markets by generating, codifying, coordinating and transferring knowledge.[6]

In general, "organisation" refers to any group, team, business unit, department, centre, community, government, charitable body, club or any other profit or non profit making unit which has more than one human entity in order to achieve collectively more complex tasks and knowledge based activities.

1.1.1. Knowledge Management (KM) – Schools of Thought–A Summary View

KM began to take shape as a distinctly new discipline during the 80's. Swedish practitioners like Karl-Erik Sveiby (and later Leif Edvinson) took note of the inadequacy of traditional measures of corporate assets. The importance of intellectual capital and the intellectual assets was recognised as also its need to be quantified.

1. Intellectual Capital: Intellectual Capital (and also Customer Capital) was recognised as an invisible asset of an Organisation. The central idea is that intellectual capital becomes the seed for commercial value. Human creativity produces innovation which can be commercialised to create commercial value. Pioneers of this approach, such as Patrick Sullivan, Gordan Petrash joined Edvinson and others to form the Intellectual Capital Movement or ICM gathering, with the declared objective of understanding how to manage invisible knowledge assets for creating value.

2. Organisational Learning: Again in the mid 80's, another group in Boston had its orientation from systems dynamics: Peter Serge of MIT, Arie de Gems of Royal Dutch Shell and Chris of Harvard – formalised itself as Centre for Organisational Learning which in

1995 became Society for Organisational Learning. These individuals concerned themselves on issues of organisational behaviour in learning – how the discipline of an organisation depends upon the way people think and relate to themselves and also how surfacing assumptions and mental models unravel the defences that block learning in an Organisation.

David Garvin of Harvard Business School held up a more practical approach to organisational learning to be linked to business results.

3. Knowledge Transfer: Effective Knowledge Transfer within an organisation is critical for KM in the organisation. As discussed elsewhere, the Knowledge Cycle comprises of sourcing/capturing/organising/storing/retrieving/sharing/transferring and finally using/reusing knowledge.

This includes benchmarking, transfer of best practices, codification of work templates and optimum use of Intranets. IT groups and engineers are oriented towards this approach and the goal is alignment of KM with business goal and results. Important centres of such activity include Carla O' Dell of American Productivity and Quality Center, Robert Buchanas of Buchanan Laboratories, Nancy Diner of George Washington University and IBM's Lawrence Purask.

4. Knowledge Innovation: There is yet another approach which believes that creating knowledge and providing the environment or means to encourage innovation in a group is more important than managing explicit or codified knowledge. In this School of KM, it is perceived that the first step in innovation is basically tacit and human processes that require different perspectives and methods.

The leading exponents of this school of KM are Ikujino Nonaka of Hitotsubashi University and UC Berkeley, George Van Krogh of University of St. Gallon in Switzerland. Dorothy Leonard of Harvard Business School, Debra Amidson of Entovation International, David Snowden of IBM Institute of KM are other such exponents. All these who know how the tacit processes and subtleties in human relationships are critical in fostering innovation while Leonard talks of "creative abrasions". Nonaka describes 'ba' or shared interpersonal space among Japanese innovation teams. David Snowden of IBM's Institute of KM has developed a model for understanding the cultural underpinnings of knowledge processes and also about story telling as part of KM. Van Krogh observed how a "caring" organisational culture nurtures technological innovation. Etienne Wanger showed how invisible informal social processes actually do facilitate knowledge sharing in real life communities of practice.

The above is the summary coverage of four schools of thought of KM.

Let us go for a deeper analysis.

1.1.2. Intellectual Capital

Knowledge-based assets or intellectual capital is now being identified as a key asset of an organisation.

"The limitless resources that can spring out of the infinite human ability to create new knowledge" is the basis for the Intellectual Capital. In contrast with other physical assets which deplete upon sharing, the intellectual capital assets grow and get enhanced when shared.

The intangible or invisible assets of a company or organisation are many times more worthy than the physical or visible assets.

Since Sreiby wrote his seminal book "The Know-How Company" in 1986, many of his colleagues had formed a group called "Intellectual Capital Movement Group".

They held that the intangible intellectual or knowledge assets should be recognised, measured and managed to create value. Prominent individuals in this movement are: Leif Edvinson, Professor of Intellectual Capital, University of Lund, Sweden. He pioneered the measurement of intellectual capital and created the world's first corporate Intellectual Capital (IC) annual report.

David Teece, Professor of International Business and Finance, University of California, Berkeley wrote the book "Managing Intellectual Capital" in 2000. Earlier, he studied commercialisation and technology innovation.

Hubert St. Onge, CEO of Kosiverge Digital Solutions, first introduced the concept of "customer capital" or "stake holder capital" or "external capital" as a component of (three) intellectual capital components.

Patrick Sullivan, a founder of ICM group focussed on how to create value from intellectual assets. He wrote "Value division intellectual capital for: How to convert intangible corporate assets into Market value" (John Wiley, 2000).

Baruch Lev, Professor of Accounting and Finance at New York University Stern School of Business. He directs the Project for Research on Intangibles".

Thomas Stewart, on Board of Editors of Fortune Magazine" wrote popular book "Intellectual Capital: The New Wealth of Organisation" (Doubleday 1997).

1.1.3. Knowledge Transfer

This school of thought believes that Knowledge Transfer is the key element essential for enhancing performance, quality and productivity.

Studies done by American Productivity and Quality Centre (APQC) showed that within an organisation, transfer of knowledge and best practices clearly results in higher productivity. Carla O Dell, the President of APQC and Jackson Gragson, Chairman APQC are the noted Champions of this school of thought of KM practice ("If only we know what we know: The Transfer of Internal Knowledge and Best Practices" Free Press 1988).

The main principle here is that transfer and reuse of knowledge creates value. But the problems according to APQC study are:

- Companies are not always aware that they possess useful knowledge.
- If companies do know, potential receivers or adopters may not be able to absorb or reuse the knowledge in the company.
- A barrier to transfer is lack of connection or relationship between the source and recipient within the same company.

Nancy Dixon ("Common Knowledge: How Companies thrive by sharing what they know" Harvard Business School Press 2000) observed that companies engage in different kinds of knowledge transfer depending on the nature of the task (frequent or non routine), kind of knowledge (tacit or explicit) and similarity between source and receiver of knowledge.

In this school of thought, the concern is about managing knowledge at various stages of knowledge cycle:

- Internal and external sensing,
- Creation, sourcing or capture and
- Sharing, applying and using/reusing.

In this approach, the knowledge cycle is linear, production-oriented and systematic.

1.1.4. Organisational Learning

Organisational learning and knowledge management are interrelated. They overlap in the difficult but challenging human dimensions affecting how knowledge is acquired in a group context.

Peter Senge's (of MIT) famous book "The Fifth Discipline: the Act and Practice of Learning Organisations" (1990) highlights the following:

- Organisations work the way they work depending on the way the people concerned think and how they interact.
- Behaviour of organisations can be understood better by using "Systems thinking" (System dynamics).

Learning in a group context required members to make explicit their unexpressed thoughts, mental models and ladders of inference.

If we cannot express our assumptions explicitly in ways that others can understand and build upon, there can be no longer a process of testing these assumptions and building public (group) knowledge – this is team dynamics.

Other important works in this school are "The Reflective Practitioner" by Jessey Bass 1987 "Overcaring Organisational Defences" by Chris Argyns. They collaborated to develop "action science" which looks at the difference between expressed values and values that actually underlie action ("Organisational Learning: a theory of Action Perspectives" Addison Wesley 1978). The central idea of this theory is the importance of unconscious "mental models" that affect how people behave and make decisions. William Isacs of MIT proposed a theory of how teams effectively inquire and decide together.

Garvin of Harvard focussed on systematising procedure applied over the stages (acquiring, interpreting and applying) and types of learning (seeing/observation or intelligence gathering, practice of experience and experimentation). Garvin complemented Senge and created a bridge between organisational learning and mainstream knowledge management.

Later "learning in action" concept in workplace was brought in. In this, we can consider procedures that transform every action in the workplace into learning process.

1.1.5. Knowledge Innovation

This school of KM emphasises on Knowledge Innovation in an organisation. They emphasise that this should attract the attention of decision-makers in all levels: corporate, organisational, social and political at national and international levels. Innovation in knowledge is essential as innovation leads to better productivity in any given environment and it also results in new product development. Innovation often spawns new enterprises and new market niches.

Innovation leads to new knowledge. Creating new knowledge is more essential than managing existing knowledge.

Better managing the existing knowledge results in productivity gains but such gains are only incremental in nature. Quantum leaps of knowledge happen with descriptive knowledge creation which may be the sum-total of many knowledge innovations or even a one large knowledge innovation.

If we examine various innovations surrounding us in our daily life, each one of them started humbly with a simple invention and then got upgraded gradually with incremental knowledge innovations. Knowledge creation always began as a tacit process, individualistic in nature. Such knowledge may or may not be a subject of Knowledge Management. It may be too individualistic, too tacit and private to be managed by any KM team outside. It is individualistic knowledge innovation development.

Japanese have a large record and experience in managing tacit knowledge. They have largest experiences in the subtle act of "managing" the tacit stages of knowledge innovation process. Companies like Sony, Matsushita, Toshiba and Honda can be found in Books written by Ikujino Nonaka.

The works are by Nonaka, et al titled "The Knowledge Creating Company: How Japanese Companies create the Dynamics of Innovation", 1995 and also "Enabling Knowledge Creation: How to unlock the mystery of tacit knowledge and release power of innovation" (both by Oxford Universities Press, 1995 and 2000). They emphasise on traditional knowledge creation practices in Japan which innovate various practices.

Debra Amidon, American innovator-entrepreneur advocates the limitless potential of ICT networks to create, synergise and apply knowledge across all roots of global boundaries. She had set up Entovation (Enterprising Innovation) International – a nested network of KM practitioners in 90 countries – to demonstrate how a global "innovation superhighway" can tap the potential. According to Amidon, Entovation illustrates "not a value chain of activities but as a system dynamic, in which intellectual capital, reputation, learning and client success continuously feel (each other), progress in building access, credibility and competency. Everyone, individuals, enterprises and nations learn from the innovations of the other. Collaboration among parties is essential and collective wisdom is the only way to create new standards, rather than simply follow best practices".

Other distinguishing features of the school are:

- Attention to "ecology": appropriate organisational culture or working environment that facilitate and encourage innovation, improvement and improvisation.
- Importance given to "sensing" capabilities for correctly seeing and interpreting internal and external events and for arriving at fresh insights that may alter business strategy.
- Commitment to "learning", nurturing competencies, processes and cultures for continuous exploration, discovery and experimentation throughout the organisation.
- People oriented management attitude and competencies for motivating people to act at their very best.

Other books recommended in this school are:

Philip Sadle's "Managing Talent" (Economist Books, 1993).

Dorothy Leonard's "Well springs of Knowledge" (Harvard Business School, 1998).

Andy Law's "Creative Company" (Job Wiley, 1998).

Mathew Kiernam "Get innovative or get dead" (Douglas and McIntyre Ltd.).

1.2. Motivation for Knowledge Management

Today all organisations are very challenged in terms of the variety of problems – delivery, efficiency and effectiveness. Knowledge Management has a solution for many of the problems. While all problems cannot be solved by Knowledge Management, the solutions to such problems do have knowledge component in them.

The following are some of the challenges being faced by modern organisations:

- Structural reform or change in the organisation calling for the change management to adopt operationally and to innovate.
- A well networked organisation, but hindered by low levels of knowledge sharing.
- A domestic organisation aiming to diversify for international operations but facing competition.
- A new organisation with knowledgeable staff who lack trust or cohesive networking amongst them.
- A veteran and mature organisation facing ageing problem, trying to cope up with organisational memory loss and knowledge loss or obsolescence.
- A well networked organisation with a strong culture of knowledge sharing and team members looking to raise their performance to higher levels.

For all this above scenarios, Knowledge Management can be of great help.

Organisations which foster efficient knowledge networks and connections, explore processes and deploy people-centric technology are leveraged to manage the complexity and the ambiguity that permeates the knowledge ecosystem–the pathways and connections between people, processes, technology and content which result in a rich web of relationships and interaction.

1.3. The Knowledge Lens

The knowledge lens is a holistic way of viewing an organisation by considering all the components of the knowledge ecosystem and the knowledge needed to achieve strategic intent. By using the knowledge lens on these components, it is possible to view them from different perspectives so as to identify the actual and potential links and relationships which were not evident.

1.4. Organisation as a Knowledge Ecosystem

In the current knowledge era, an organisation can be considered as an ecosystem that consists of a complex set of interactions amongst people, processes, technology and content – various entities in the ecosystem.

In such knowledge ecosystem, there is a path from information to knowledge to value by making use of individuals or groups. The knowledge-enabled organisation considers people and their knowledge as the primary assets (unlike the conventional model in Industrial Management where people behave as commodities in a command and control environment).

The knowledge ecosystem of an organisation can be viewed through the knowledge lens as follows:

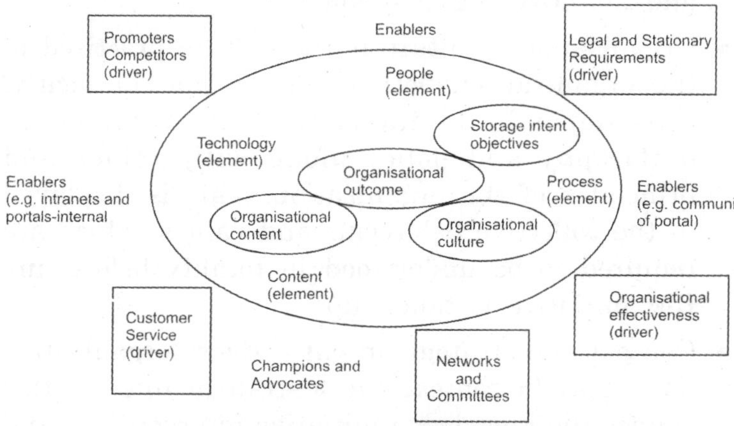

Fig. 1.1: The Knowledge Ecosystem.

The main core of the knowledge eco-system (as above) is the organisational outcome. This flows from the contextual environment (organisational culture and strategic intent) and the manner in which the organisation operates, given its business environment.

1.4.1. Aim of Knowledge Management in the Knowledge Ecosystem of the Organisation

The major aim of Knowledge Management in an organisation is to stimulate and enhance the collective organisational skills and competencies within the organisation. To begin with, a deep understanding has to be gained on why knowledge management should be implemented and where in the organisation it should start. For example, it is not correct to start with Intranets and internal portals, simply as technological tools without the corresponding content being prepared internally. Similarly, the effectiveness of the linkages people have with such tools (as Intranets and internal portals) has to be ensured before actually developing and operating any such tools.

As in the above diagram (Fig. 1.1), the specific components of knowledge ecosystem are:

- Organisational outcomes are the business objectives which aim at creating an innovative and adaptive organisation.
- Organisational culture is the culture practised in the organisation, both explicitly and implicitly. This depends on the management direction, philosophy and policy along with values and principles of the organisation. This is displayed in the collective behaviour and values, which are required to be understood in totality before any KM initiative is taken up.
- Context and strategic intent – Every organisation has a specific context and a strategic intent – this shapes the knowledge initiative interventions and knowledge management. Knowledge intensive organisations have critical knowledge management requirements. Any knowledge intervention such as (Knowledge Management initiative) should be guided and moulded by this context and align with the strategic intent. Finally, when successfully effective, every knowledge management initiative has the ability to drive the strategic intent and alter the organisational context accordingly.

- Drivers are driving forces.
- Elements – The four elements are – People, Process, Technology and Content – they are present in all organisations. Appropriate balance has to be maintained across all the four – disproportionate emphasis on one or two can lead to imbalance in the organisation.
- Enablers are specific activities, tools or techniques that populate the ecosystem. The combination of enablers which will have effective impact depends on the structures in the organisation – the organisational capability, culture, content and strategic intent.
- Networks and communities are social configurations. They may be voluntary, self-organising and may adapt common tools, symbols, signs, artifacts, stories and histories, as they evolve and reach maturity. Knowledge flows between people involved in such network and communities and it surfaces in conversations, discussions and interactions.
- Champions and advocates are people who actively promote knowledge-based activities, knowledge adoption and its use. These people provide the guidance, feedback, visibility, legitimacy and also resources for knowledge based activities to flourish and deliver results in the organisation.

1.4.2. Implementing Knowledge Management interventions – The Map/Build/Operationalise Cycle

Till now, we have seen the organisation through a knowledge lens and have also explored the knowledge ecosystem. How to implement the Knowledge Management interventions within the ecosystem?

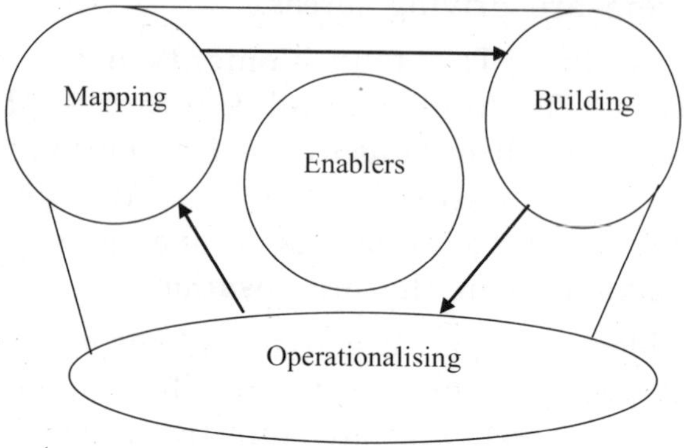

Fig. 1.2: The Cycle of Mapping, Building and Operationalising.

Each stage can be visited and revisited, according to the needs from time to time – the Enablers play a critical role to support these phases. Let us analyse each of these phases:

Mapping: The Mapping phase focuses on setting the background and the context for knowledge management.

It calls for the investigation and analysis of the knowledge ecosystem.

Building: In the building phase, adequate motivation is required to be given to the actors in the organisation to experiment with the new ideas in KM and pilot knowledge interventions. In this phase, the focus is on building experience and linkages between people, processes, technology and content.

Operationalising : In this phase, the focus shifts from experimenting and building to implementing and operationalising. It my involve, for example, rolling out selected pilots for large scale implementation.

The Enablers are at the centre and are used in all phases, i.e., Map/Build/Operationalise cycles. While these may be varying activities, there are certain common characteristics of the Map/Build/Operate cycle as:

- the state of readiness in knowledge ecosystem of the organisation.
- the scalability of each phase of the cycle.
- the ability to build a long-term, sustainable organisational capacity to respond to knowledge ecosystem.
- the continuous nature of the phase.

1.5. Conclusion

To conclude, in this chapter we have defined Knowledge Management (KM) in an organisation. We have analysed and understood what is knowledge lens and its role in knowledge ecosystem of the organisation. The role of enablers to populate and activate knowledge ecosystem has been identified. The Map/Build/Operate cycle is presented as a framework to implement knowledge interventions in an organisation.

References

1. Anthes G H (1991), "A Step Beyond a Database", Computer World, Vol. 25, No. 9, p. 28.
2. Davenport T H (1994), "Coming Soon: The CKO", Information Week, September.
3. Nonaka I and Takeuchi H (1994), "A Dynamic Theory of Organisational Knowledge Creation", Organisational Science, Vol. 5, No. 1, pp. 14-37.
4. O'Dell C (1996), "A Current Review of Knowledge Management Best Practices: Conference of Knowledge Management and the Transfer of Best Practices", Business Intelligence, London.
5. Malhotra Y (1998), "Knowledge Management for the New World of Business", Journal for Quality and Participation, July-August, pp. 58-60, available www.brint.com/km/whatis.htm, accessed on August, 2002.
6. Davenport T H and Prusak L (1998), Working Knowledge: How Organisations Manage What They Know, Harvard Business School Press, Boston.

2

Knowledge Mapping

The Mapping phase of Knowledge Management (KM) focuses on setting the context for KM. It comprises investigation and full understanding of the knowledge ecosystem.

Firstly, a proper vision definition should be made for Knowledge Management. The vision should clearly bring out the motivation for KM in terms of the necessity and benefits with a force of vision which shall generate enthusiasm among all the stake holders. To make this happen, various enablers are to be identified and stimulated to ensure the execution.

During the mapping phase, the gaps in knowledge are required to be identified. It also comprises of identifying what knowledge – in terms of people, process, technology and content – will enable it to identify knowledge gaps and achieve the strategic interest of the organisation.

The Mapping phase can scale across the entire enterprise or a particular department or unit, or can even be limited to one or more particular business processes (e.g., project management).

The first step is to identify the status of knowledge in the target organisational unit/business process (i.e., knowledge ecosystem). The second step is to define the strategic interest of the organisation – where the organisation wants to be? The third step is to identify the gap between one and two above. Fourth step is to draw a map of the targetted knowledge ecosystem – the goal. Finally we have to identify the processes and modified (old) processes required to achieve the target knowledge ecosystem as per the strategic interest of the organisation.

Accordingly, the top management has to initiate executive action with full ownership and commitment.

2.1. The Methodology of Mapping

The knowledge ecosystem model shown in the Fig. 1.1 previously (in Chapter 1) focuses on the organisational outcomes.

With a clear understanding of the organisational outcomes aimed to be achieved, using the knowledge ecosystem as the background, the content of the organisation has to be well understood, in order to build a clear map of opportunities and constraints for activating knowledge in the organisation. While performing this exercise, the key consideration or questions will be as:

1. Identity and the nature of the organisation (public/private/profit making/non-profit making).
2. What are the government and other regulations or Acts affecting/controlling the organisation (e.g., company law, public sector regulations, audit process, Right to Information Act, etc.).
3. Structure of the organisation (formal/informal) – organisational hierarchy chart to be provided.
4. What are the ethics and values of the organisation?
5. Where the specific individual interests of various stake holders (e.g., government / partners or shareholders / public, etc.).

6. Strengths and weaknesses of the organisation.
7. Competition to the organisation.
8. What are the relevant trends in political environment or international relations?
9. What are the effects of globalisation on the organisation?
10. Any other important information about the organisation.

The objective in such an analysis is to gain clear understanding of the implications of the strategic context for knowledge interaction which induce a desired strong change.

- What is the strategic interest of the organisation, its vision statement, mission statement, goals and action plans?
- What are the goals the organisation is trying to achieve?
- SWOT Analysis of the organisation. SWOT stands for Strengths, Weaknesses, Opportunities and Threats.
- How the top management is trying to articulate strategic interest?

By the above analysis, external processes or Drivers can be identified and understood. By analysing the Drivers through the knowledge lens, we can understand the impact of Drivers on knowledge ecosystem and their constraints and also possible outcomes.

2.2. Existing Knowledge Ecosystem

Mapping can be taken up either for the entire organisation or for a single business unit (or department) or even only on a single business process.

2.2.1. How to Perform Mapping of an Existing Knowledge System?

By using a "knowledge lens" for looking at:

(a) people,

(b) process,

(c) technology, and

(d) context,

the following questions have to be answered:

(i) Who knows what?

(ii) How the sharing of knowledge happens?

(iii) How knowledge flows?

(iv) Who creates the knowledge and where?

(v) Where the knowledge is disseminated or received?

(vi) Which knowledge is valuable?

(vii) Which knowledge is critical?

(viii) Which critical knowledge is missing?

The answers to the above questions also depend upon the culture of the organisation which is responsible for the thinking traits, attitudes, behaviour and perceptions of individuals and groups.

For determining the above, it is useful to analyse the Related Areas of Practice (RAP) in the organisation and the work they are involved in (see Appendix on Related Area of Practice). For executing or supporting any knowledge initiative, the potential of leveraging the skills, initiatives and practices has to be considered.

2.3. Enablers for Knowledge Analysis

The enabler which helps in identifying the existing knowledge and how knowledge flows (or does not flow) via the relationships between people in the knowledge ecosystem are:

(a) Auditing of knowledge (generation, flow and vacuum).

(b) Auditing of information (generation, flow and vacuum).

(c) Mapping of knowledge.

(d) Survey of organisational culture and climate.

(e) Analysis of social networks.

Analysis of social networking brings out the hidden or shadow knowledge flows in the organisation. Such flows will usually run in a direction opposite to those shown in organisational chart.

2.4. Knowledge Management Maturity Model (KMMM)

Any organisation evolves in its knowledge management dimension. The evolution is always from simple or little maturity to advanced state of maturity. Very similar to other maturity models (e.g., SEI's CMM for software), the Knowledge Management Maturity Model also has four states of evolution in their complexity order:

(a) "Stand alone" organisation.

(b) Connected organisation.

(c) Networked organisation.

(d) Adaptive organisation.

Let us examine each of these states of organisation:

(a) "Stand alone" organisation: In a "stand alone" organisation, the individuals and groups in the organisation work in an isolated mode. They work independently and with minimal or rare interaction. Groups in the organisation do not have effective links of communication (even through within the group, the individuals may be well connected). Thus, very little knowledge, if at all, flows across the organisation. Evidently, this is the least evolved organisation in Knowledge Management.

(b) Connected organisation: Connections are established between groups or departments and they do result in sharing of knowledge. Even though most knowledge dissemination tends to occur in a top-down manner, there exist some project teams who share knowledge related to the projects.

(c) Networked organisation : In this organisation, such knowledge networks are formed around specific domains of knowledge. Such networks may be based on specific professional interests within the organisation. These networks facilitate sharing not only of knowledge, but also experience and expertise. During their frequent or periodical meetings, they investigate new issues and problems and help create new knowledge. In such a networked organisation, the networks so established may overflow beyond the limits of the organisation, getting networked with other stake holders as well (e.g., Suppliers, Clients, Customers).

(d) Adaptive organisation : The organisation which is well equipped with knowledge will automatically become adaptive to the needs of the external environment. It shall acquire new knowledge required, thereby adapt to the demands of the external environments, including the stake holders. In such an organisation, the structures are fluid and the organisation is agile enough to adapt to the external environment. The strong internal capacity is enhanced by the continuous interaction with the external experts, thereby including them also into the network. Such an agile network can be extended, modified or reconfigured at will, as per the demands of the external environment. Evidently, such an organisation shall be the most effective and efficient in its line of business. Success is automatic for such an organisation, as the knowledge and the work (with its results) will be fully aligned with strategic interest and strategic plan.

Any given organisation can be identified with one of the four above categories. Some of the organisations may be in intermediate states also, tending towards one of these four states, eventually. However, any organisation has to evolve in the forward direction in this line.

The goal of Knowledge Management in an organisation may not necessarily to make the organisation "perfect" or reach the fourth state of "Adaptive" organisation. The magnitude of such an effort and its cost may or may not be worthwhile or even feasible, given the strategic intent of the organisation. However, the slow evolution in these states may be possible through Knowledge Management initiatives.

Skipping the states is not recommended. Gradual evolution is recommended. "Slow and steady wins the race".

2.5. Results of Mapping Phase

Mapping phase concerns itself with acquiring a deep understanding of the knowledge ecosystem of the organisation. This helps in formulating the strategy and plan for Knowledge Management for the organisation. The identified gap between the existing state and the desired state of knowledge ecosystem of the organisation helps in:

(a) setting goals,

(b) setting priorities,

(c) making a strategy for improvement and

(d) making a plan for KM implementation and operationalisation.

Such strategic goals could be:

(a) promoting knowledge sharing,

(b) building linkage to faster knowledge transfer, and

(c) improving innovation, knowledge creation and sharing.

Action steps for achieving the above could be:

(a) specific knowledge interventions,

(b) sustainable KM strategy well integrated into the ethos of the organisation,

(c) enhancing and leveraging existing knowledge environment, and

(d) starting new initiatives in the knowledge to fill the gaps.

2.6. Conclusion

In this chapter, we have presented the Methodology of Mapping of the existing knowledge eco system. We have also presented in brief the Knowledge Management Maturity Model (KMMM). Finally, we concluded with an analysis of the results of such Mapping. In the next chapter, we shall examine the "Build" phase.

3

Building Phase for KM

The mapping phase (as discussed in Chapter 2) will provide adequate information on the priorities and prepare the decisions on the appropriate approval to take the necessary action to be taken for translating the identified priorities into actionable steps. This phase is known as Building (or Action) phase, which is the second in the cycle: map/build/operationalise.

3.1. Activities for KM Intervention

What are the activities required for introducing KM into the organisation? The following could be some such activities:

(i) identify specific knowledge interventions by identifying the appropriate communities and seeding them,

(ii) developing a formal knowledge management plan,

(iii) identifying and executing the extensions into the existing knowledge infrastructure,

(iv) setting up core KM team,

(v) setting up linkages between complementary areas of KM practice,

(vi) defining and executing pilots and prototypes,

(vii) knowledge champions – identifying and promoting,

(viii) developing innovative products, processes and services.

In the map/build/operationalise cycle, the Build (or Action) phase examines how the organisation can be made a "learning organisation", into an increasingly innovative work with new ideas and pilot knowledge interventions. It is crucial phase for the following:

(a) taking action on knowledge priorities identified in the (first) mapping phase,

(b) encouraging new explorations and innovations in the organisation,

(c) distinguishing between KM interventions which work and which do not,

(d) identifying, creating and encouraging knowledge, and

(e) develop pilots and prototypes.

3.2. Evolution of KM in the Organisation

KM can falter or collapse at the critical point of being translated from ideas into action. Why KM interventions can fail or fail to deliver to the expected levels? Any of the following could be the reason for this:

(a) poor fitting between adopted Elements and Enablers, and organisational culture and context,

(b) introducing the new Enablers in the organisation without laying the appropriate foundation and ground work for their success,

(c) lack of collaboration with related practice as records and information management and IT, and

(d) failing to reflect the organisation's dominant culture mix in the implementation plan.

Very few plans of KM survive the implementation intact. This building or action phase helps to probe.

3.3. Enablers

How to select the Enablers for KM? In the previous Mapping phase, the knowledge gaps and the priorities that needed to be addressed were identified. These gaps indicate the Enablers required for bridging the gaps. These Enablers are required to be introduced during the current Building phase.

From the Mapping phase, the skills, tools and techniques present in different areas of practice in the organisation are also identified. Apart from selecting new Enablers, we may also partner and work with these related areas of practice to strengthen and support existing knowledge activities. It is essential that the selected enablers be in line with the strategic intent, culture and context of the organisation. It is also essential that a balance is maintained across the four Elements, ensuring that knowledge gaps are addressed.

Organisational culture is a critical issue for KM. It shapes the content of communications and the contextual environment in which work is done and knowledge is created, shared and applied. Every organisation has its own unique culture that evolves over time through cumulative interactions with wider ecosystems and relationships between people and their environment. Organisational culture is the social and behavioural glue that binds an organisation.

In this Building phase, experimenting with knowledge interventions is a way of customising the Enablers to suit the existing cultural nuances and ensuring that knowledge reflects the organisational context.

When we understand clearly what exactly works in the organisation as per its culture, we can then execute the implementation of KM effectively and also efficiently.

3.4. Prototyping and Pilot Projects

Pilots and Prototypes become valuable if not critical requirements for successfully implementing a KM in an organisation. Pilots provide the organisation with an opportunity to develop hands-on familiarity and confidence with Enablers. Practical experience gained pilots provides the credibility and commitment with confidence and also broadens the organisation's capabilities by creating an interval pool of expertise.

Pilots are not the same as Prototypes. A Pilot is a discrete and manageable project that typically has duration of four to six months after which its performance is evaluated. A Prototype is a small system with restricted scope and functionality built for a Pilot. A Prototype is often referred to as a "PoC" (Proof of Concept).

Both Pilots and Prototypes enable a mean of better understanding how an Enabler will fit with the organisational culture and context.

Pilots and Prototypes also have their weakness points. They are frequently functioning, involving good amount of trial and error. Successful pilots require patience, flexibility and a willingness to respond to the organisational need, context and scope.

A Pilot need not be representative, especially when the total domain is large. Variations can be substantial on the ground. Therefore, usually one pilot may not be sufficient. Several pilots in several geographical or cultural zones in the domain may have to be executed to gain adequate insight into the real issues, problems and constraints. This rich experience of multiple pilots enables a large roll out in the entire organisation. Such experience can rapidly cascade throughout the organisation through champions and advocates.

3.5. Building Organisational Structures and Linkages

Organisational teams and structures are required to adopt organic adaptive forms to deliver pilots and prototypes. The skills concerned may be located in a central group or can be brought together, as needed, within a cross functional team.

A key skilled worker or manager, who can connect one or more networks and still work outside the network boundaries, plays a crucial role in the direction of KM initiatives. He facilitates the knowledge sharing and he strengthens social networks, which in turn help the organisation to make sense of its surrounding ecosystem. Such persons and teams spur innovations and convey competitive advantage by introducing new knowledge, new technologies, new interactions, and new networks to the organisation.

In the Build phase, all these linkages are built across different areas of the organisations and its external stake holders.

3.6. Communicating Knowledge Intervention

Communication is very critical in KM interventions. By effective communication of the benefits of knowledge activities, we can build a high level of awareness and support. Effective communication can generate trust: an integral requirement for KM.

Brand and image building of a KM programme is essential to draw adequate attention from the stake holders. Brands supported by logos, icons and themes create emotional links and cues between the participants and KM interventions. Intranets, portals, communities of practice and collaboration spaces are all very effective tools for KM initiatives.

Above efforts will foster performance and sustainability by humanising technology and personalising group spaces. Outcomes will be higher awareness levels and increased use of Enablers.

3.7. Building Champions, Advocates, Promoters, Mandate and Organisational Competitiveness

Creating internal champions and advocates is essential part of the build phase. Champions and internal advocates are effective means of building interest and demand for new tools and techniques. All these finally pave the way for an organisational mandate for a particular KM intervention by demonstrating its tangible value and clarifying its associated costs, resource requirements and deployment complexity.

The existing core and non-core competencies of the organisation have to be developed and strengthened, while the new competencies can be developed in the Build phase. Such new competencies may be essential for KM intervention, as pre-requisites. On the other hand, new KM initiatives can also result in new competencies in new areas. Such skills are developed in fielding pilots, building new prototypes, inspiring and nurturing champions, developing crucial teams and fostering social network.

Additional and/or complementary competencies include:

Innovation and Ideation,

Business Process Redesign and Reengineering,

Change Management,

Coaching and Mentoring, and

Influencing and negotiating.

3.8. Resistance Management

KM intervention may generate some resistance. Organisational resistance originates from fear of failure or the fear of the unknown, in addition to confronting nature of learning new skills. Identifying important business is essential as:

- Adding work load,

- Lack of trust between members,
- Rewarding knowledge hoarding instead of sharing,
- Knowledge experts being unwilling, and
- KM seen as trans-disciplinary.

3.9. Outcomes of Build Phase

The new and improved Enablers, Capabilities are the outcomes of Build phase, as:

- what does not work and what works?,
- how to innovate?,
- better understanding of change implementation,
- better and deeper understanding of culture and organisational structure, and
- streamlining pilots and improving cycle times.

Conclusion

The Build phase, with its emphatic role in developing skills and experience around activating knowledge, prepares for an ongoing program of operationalising and embedding KM intervention and the Enablers in the organisational framework.

4

Operationalisation

After the Map and Build phases of KM intervention, Operationalisation becomes the logical consequence and last stage. This is expected to leverage the opportunities existing within the knowledge ecosystem of the organisation. This final phase naturally depends upon and is drawn on the experiences, capabilities, competencies and linkages gained in the Build Phase.

This phase of operationalisation is meant for:

(a) Rolling out proven pilots,
(b) Strengthening enablers,
(c) Collaborative working practice,
(d) Coordinating with all other KM interventions,
(e) Commercialising the knowledge products, if possible, and
(f) Ensuring widespread acceptance of KM, in general and KM interventions, in particular.

4.1. Operationalisation of Knowledge and Knowledge Management Initiatives and Interventions

In the operationalisation phase, the most important consideration is the feasibility: what works for the organisation? Earlier interventions and initiatives which were tested as pilots are required to be realised in a total roll-out and grounding in this phase of operationalisation. Many critical issues may crop up in this phase – many problems and bottlenecks unforeseen during the pilots may become evident and even dominant. Solutions to such problems are required to be worked out in this phase. Key decisions are required to be made about:

the scale of roll-out – scalability issues such as options as incremental expansion versus full blast roll-out as "Big Hit",

phasing various interventions so as to ensure cohesion and complementary with each other and not contradiction, and

appropriate relation of enablers – as per the provision of the organisation.

4.2. Operational Environments

Operational environment for roll-out should have certain specific characteristics: it should be orderly, disciplined and often highly-structured. New explorations or investigations have to be eliminated. This will reduce risks, avoid wastage, enable cost savings and status monitoring and predictability, reliability and scalability across the enterprise. Leveraging on previous experiences will reduce the adoption cycle of the intervention. Isolated pilots are usually raised to an operational level to form programmes. Associating the relevant skills and expertise with the initiation accelerates the speed of knowledge transfer with "leap frogging" effect. The other aspects which are to be considered are:

(i) Change Management aspects,

(ii) Project Management aspects,

(iii) Training, and

(iv) Monitoring and evaluation.

4.3. Branding and its Benefits

As discussed in previous chapter, effective branding plays a very crucial role in any knowledge initiative even in the operationalisation phase. Additional and effective communication around the objectives, benefits and values of the knowledge initiatives is required. Branding, comprising an effective positioning of an intervention, along with appropriate imaging is crucial for success. In addition to the word of mouth, more formal communication mechanisms will be very beneficial.

4.4. Operational Champions, dvocates and Mandate

The champions and advocates of the build phase have a profound role to play even in the operationalisation phase. Instead of just acting as minimum role champions in the operationalisation phase, the champions play more extensive role in motivating the teams to participate in knowledge interventions and adapt them as their own. Champions play a dominant role in the operationalisation phase not only in motivating others but also own up the entire roll out of the intervention by engaging in monitoring and regulating the roll out, adapting and owning the whole intervention as their own.

The Mandate of Build phase becomes the charter agenda in the operationalisation phase. Champions play a day-to-day role in nurturing and sustaining it. Organisational mandates from top level are also required in this phase. Advocates are a rich source of testimonials for the interventions which further strengthen the mandate from the top.

4.5. Competencies and Skills in Operationalisation

Whatever skills and competencies were developed during the Build phase can be extended into operationalisation phase, which calls for a variety of skill and competency spectrum of many disciplies as:

Change Management – identifying levels of change (including cultural issues and operational risks).

Influencing and Negotiating Skills – Creating demand for the Knowledge intervention and also generating a mandate.

Communication and relationship building – creating a shared understanding of the knowledge intervention.

Technology – training and understanding of the capabilities and limitations of the technology in implementing the intervention.

Project Management – identifying key dependencies in knowledge and also identifying linkages of knowledge.

Financial analysis – A measurement regime for KM.

BPR – Business Process Reengineering for improved performance, avoiding wastages.

The above competencies (and some more) can also be interpreted in different ways.

4.6. Sustainability Beyond Operationalisation Phase

KM has to be a sustainable and ongoing activity. Knowledge connects and integrates the organisation, its activities and functions. Therefore, the sustainability of knowledge interventions beyond the operationalisation stage is critical for success. The following steps can help sustain any knowledge intervention:

(a) Publicising the new way of doing things across the organisation,

(b) Embedding the new knowledge-based activities

in existing business practices and systems,

(c) Connecting and leveraging knowledge activities across various areas of related practice (e.g., HR and competitive evaluations),

(d) Continued skill and capability development through training and retraining,

(e) Maintaining champions and mandates,

(f) Taking feedback on the implementation phase, and

(g) Using the feedback of operationalisation to revisit Build phase mandates to ensure sensitivity to the changing organisational context over a period of time.

4.7. Indications of Success

There are many ways in which the success of a knowledge intervention can be measured:

(a) Item-centric indicators indicate changed or improved use of new items and artifacts such as documents, video/audio files, images, etc.

(b) Activity-centric indicators such as improved consulting, coaching, mentoring, training, etc. and

(c) cultural or behavioural change-indicators such as altered behaviour of the individuals and organisational units, etc., as can be observed evidently.

4.8. Conclusion

In this chapter, we have presented the purpose, process and conclusion of the (third) operationalisation phase of the KM interventions and initiatives.

5

Critical Success Factors

A learning organisation alone can survive the competitive environment. Organisational learning is a reflective process, to be executed by all members (in all levels) of the organisation. This process involves collecting information, filtering it and sharing the interpretations that can be used to initiate action resulting in enduring changes in the behaviour of the organisation.

In the previous chapters, the process of implementing Knowledge Management (KM) has been presented. In this chapter, we shall examine the considerations pertaining to various critical factors involved in a successful KM implementation. What are the critical factors for a successful KM implementation? We can identify the following:

(i) Status and maturity level of IT implementation in the organisation,

(ii) Status and maturity of Knowledge Repository creation and management,

(iii) Organisational culture,

(iv) Motivation level of the Top Management for KM implementation,

(v) Motivation level of the Employees (at all levels) for KM implementation, and

(vi) Human resources.

Let us examine each of these central factors for success in KM.

5.1. Status and Maturity Level of IT Implementation in the Organisation

KM has a lot in common with IT implementation. A good extent of KM is done, if IT implementation is of a high standard, along with its documentation. For example, ISO: 9001 based documentation of IT systems in the organisation automatically provides the basis and grounds for KM implementation in the organisation. In addition, the tools for KM are essentially IT tools as:

(a) IT tools which support knowledge sharing,

(b) IT tools which support knowledge distribution, and

(c) IT tools which support knowledge capture and codification.

Without the above tools, it is not practically possible to execute KM implementation in the organisation. The above tools act as the essential infrastructure for KM implementation.

What are the risks involved in such implementation? The KM implementation team members may not have a clear vision of technology and tools which will be used for KM implementation in the organisation. They need to be well trained, in advance, on these tools. This will ensure that KM implementation team will not design a plan of implementation which will be over-running the existing IT tool infrastructure. Security issues also will have to be taken care by providing for the existing security measures available in the tools.

However, the IT tools have their own limitations. Human interactions cannot be replaced or substituted by IT tools. Brainstorming, aiming at new ideas and novel solutions is purely a human activity. IT tools will only help in implementing the best practices evolved by human interactions based on practical experience. Most projects are concerned with transfer of best practices and knowledge repositories using IT tools. The challenge lies in the use of the ability to use appropriate IT tools to bring new knowledge into the organisation and transfer it to new products and business models.

5.2. Knowledge Repositories[1]

Knowledge Repositories comprise knowledge embedded in documents, memos, e-mails, articles, presentations, etc,. They should be created (independent of people who created them) such that knowledge can be easily retrieved from such repositories. Invaluable knowledge resides in the minds of people i.e., tacit knowledge. Such knowledge has to be put into a structured and easily retrievable form. The critical factor for success in KM projects is to find the right balance of structures to represent knowledge. Lack of definite structures makes its retrievability a difficult task. Organisations which build knowledge repositories should be based on key terms and categories in a standard manner, so that the search and retrieval processes become easy.

Another important issue is the evolutionary nature of knowledge itself. Knowledge cannot remain static – it evolves with time. New knowledge becomes current and old knowledge becomes obsolete. Therefore, a Knowledge Management repository becomes obsolete very fast. Knowledge managers should play a critical role in updating the knowledge repository by loading new capital and refreshing the outdated knowledge. Without such activity, the knowledge repository will soon become dysfunctional causing the organisation substantial loss of cost and its decisions will be based on outdated knowledge. Creating knowledge silos and powerhouses (knowledge warehouses) accompanied by periodic information auditing would help the organisation in managing and extracting the required knowledge.

5.3. Organisational Culture[2]

Culture is defined as the "collective programming of the mind". Culture is also understood as a shared system of perceptions and values of a group or organisation who share such perceptions and values. Organisational culture is a key element in managing organisational change and renewal. In knowledge management, the organisational culture or climate is the most important factor. Changing organisational culture is also possible through appropriate knowledge management. Organisations which fail to shift cultural attitudes will not remain knowledge focused and any efforts in KM may not succeed or only be giving short lived results.

Human elements embedded in a culture are determinants of effective business performance and change management. The changes must address any conflict between the individual and group interests and the manner of structure: power, authority and control within the organisation.

Organisational culture plays a very important role in a Knowledge Management Project as its boundaries may restrict the flow of information and knowledge amongst the employees. Such restrictions may be affecting certain employees who may resist such changes. One of the critical factors of success for a KM Project is that the employees should be willing to share their knowledge with others and also utilise the knowledge available with others.

A knowledge centered organisational culture will force the people to share knowledge throughout the organisation. A culture of confidence and trust is required to encourage the development and application of knowledge within the organisation (Moffett et al 2002). Organisational culture is reflected in style of management, organisational operations and working practices in the organisation. Cultural bottlenecks can be overcome by "changing the mindset" of the employees and educating the employees within the organisation. For creating an environment of acceptance, the benefits of Knowledge Management should be highlighted as ease of work, reduction of work load, and better productivity.

So the critical factor for success in Knowledge Management Project is to create a conducive organisational culture and precise policies that promote sharing of knowledge and encourage the employees to help others.

5.4. Top Management Commitment

Success of KM project is critically dependent on the quantum of commitment by the top management. If the top management feels the need for KM, then they will implement KM. If they do not feel the urgency or priority or need for KM, then KM project will never be successfully implemented in the organisation.

The Knowledge Managers and the KM team should communicate to the top management the added values and the necessity of KM implementation efforts so as to convince the top management. If the top management is convinced, it will have to convince the entire organisation of the need and importance of KM. They should instill in their employees the importance and the benefits of KM. Top Management sponsorship without active ongoing involvement is a bottleneck in achieving success in KM Projects. Therefore, it is not adequate to have top management commitment in the beginning along – it is to be sustained and continuously be seen to exist during the actual implementation of KM. The support and sponsorship from top management is to be continuously checked and ensured to be continuously delivered in a practical and public way. Top Management commitment is evident from its public statements of policy and also the funding and infrastructure support for KM Projects, as also in actual statement of specifications of knowledge content for KM implementation.

A top management that is truly committed to KM would create a knowledge-oriented culture and support changes in performance measurement.

5.5. Motivation of Employees

Knowledge is in individual's possession. Therefore, knowledge is inextricably tied up with individual's ego and ownership. Knowledge is bound to the individual occupation and it does not flow easily across functional and occupational boundaries.

Therefore, the presence of motivation to create, share and use knowledge is an intangible critical success factor for any knowledge management project. How to generate motivation amongst employees for knowledge management activities? This is the real challenge always.[3] What are the incentives for knowledge workers? Are such incentives going to work? If pride and satisfaction are the real motivators in the intrinsic level, then how extrinsic incentives will help? Recognition and appreciation by the peers, not financial rewards, are the prime motivations in community participation. People who contribute regularly to the organisation or community want their contribution to be recognised by the organisation or community. Quantity based incentives may result in low quality contribution in large members to avail such incentives. Real high quality contribution comes out when the commitment is there within ownership and high level of motivation. Cultural factors in an organisation have to change so that people are rewarded for sharing information rather than holding to it. The real challenge of KM is to ensure that knowledge sharing is rewarded instead of knowledge holding.

Financial rewards to an employee every time to share his/her knowledge with a colleague (or deliver a lecture or course) may be expensive, impossible to monitor and evaluate and would also encourage narrow minded behaviour. Appropriate incentive structures which do not cause conflicts between people, projects, departments, offices, time and budget need to be introduced. Therefore, incentive has been identified as one of the critical success factor for any KM project. A performance based review is better where an individual's contribution to the organisation will be recorded and evaluated.[4]

KM being a strategic objective, appropriate by chosen incentives alone can bring in the desired results. Employees need to be rewarded for sustaining a healthy organisational climate and sharing their knowledge. Employees should be motivated to exchange knowledge as a matter of organisational culture, with due recognition as incentives (Financial incentives are not adequate motivation). Such recognition should become a part of performance evaluation and assessment.

The inclusion of senior management in the KM efforts will provide additional motivation for the staff to share the knowledge and increase chances of success in KM practice. Adequate understanding of the commitment and motivation of knowledge workers will help in alleviating the "knowledge application gap". Appropriate and adequate motivation to the employees increases their commitment levels and hence KM projects become a part of the routine activities in the organisation.

5.6. Human Resources[4, 5]

All organisations, which are knowledge-based or knowledge-intensive, critically depend on their human resources. Successful implementation of new technologies is dependent on many factors, including efficient management of employees in the organisation. Knowledge treasures lie within the organisations in the form of human capital (Soliman and Spooner 2000). The organisation should implement a strategy to harness the knowledge of the employees. If found lacking, the up gradation of knowledge should be done, as required. Employee participation is essential for KM Project implementation. Employees should own the KM Project implementation on their own.

In every knowledge-based organisation, it is essential to ensure that individual knowledge is first upgraded to up-to-date levels and then disseminated from such individuals to all others in the organisation. This means, firstly, such individuals have to be identified, who are capable and willing to disseminate their up-to-date knowledge to their other colleagues in the organisation through training programmes/ workshops. This way knowledge dissemination becomes successful and inexpensive. The other alternative is to train each and every member of the organisation through the external training faculty – an expensive and sometimes infeasible solution.

Recruitment has a major role to play in knowledge management. A potential employee should be screened for not only the professional competencies but also for creative problem-solving abilities and an inherent aptitude and capability for learning and also sharing knowledge with others (5).

Any Knowledge Management Project should have clearly defined objectives, adequate resources and focus on knowledge along with team spirit and team orientation (3).

Correct team identification for KM implementation is critical. KM Project teams are required not only to improve the performance and standing of the enterprise but also to ensure the effectiveness of the regular KM practice resulting out of the KM Project implementation. The team members should be very competent and fully conscious of the various dimensions of KM in the organisation; they should be able to control and manage a project effectively and pass it safe through crisis and solve all kinds of bottlenecks.

Critical factors which hold back the success of KM in an organisation are:

(a) Knowledge is embedded in people and knowledge creation and dissemination occurs in the process of social interaction (either in real world or in cyber space),

(b) Knowledge resides in the user and not in the collection of information. Therefore, the manner and methodology with which the user interacts with knowledge base determines knowledge dissemination,

(c) Therefore, creating appropriate supportive environment for knowledge management projects enables employees to spend time on knowledge sharing,

(d) Changes in organisational culture demands employees to change their mindsets and break with past traditions, and

(e) Organisations should facilitate various fora as staff meetings for knowledge management activities, change lay out of staff seating, create trust among employees to improve knowledge sharing.

5.7. Conclusion

This chapter has presented some of the key critical success factors for KM Project implementation in an organisation. They are:

(i) Organisational culture for knowledge sharing among the employees,

(ii) Technology, i.e., IT tools for KM implementation – their utilisation but not over dependence upon them,

(iii) Employee motivation in KM Projects and various incentives to enhance it,

(iv) Human Resource Development (HRD) activity in the organisation so as to share knowledge,

(v) Creation and maintenance of Knowledge Repositories in the Organisation, and

(vi) Sustainable and visible top management commitment including active involvement, funding and infrastructure support.

Only future research will indicate the impact of some more issues on KM as: knowledge recycling, project management, process management and budget.

References

1. Davenport H, De Long and Been C (1998) "Successful KM Projects" Sloan Management Review Vol. 34. Nov. pp. 43-57.
2. Solap M and Pandey V (2003) "Culture as an Issue in Knowledge sharing: A Means of Competitive Advantage", Elections Journal of Knowledge Management", Vol. 1, Issue 2, pp. 205-212.
3. Moffett et al (2002): "Developing a Model for Technology and cultural factors in Knowledge Management: A factor Analysis" Journal of Knowledge and Process Management (Electronic), Vol. 9, No. 4, pp. 237-255.
4. Birkinshaw J (2001): "Why is Knowledge Management so difficult" Business Strategy Review, Vol. 12, Issue 1, pp. 11-18.
5. Wichett A and Herschell J (2001): "Knowledge Management Issues for Smaller Businesses", Journal of KM (Electronic), Vol. 5, No. 4, pp. 329-337.

6

Enablers for Knowledge Management (KM)

In this chapter, we shall discuss about Enablers (or enabling factors) for Knowledge Management. Such Enablers can be tools, techniques and other activities useful in implementing Knowledge Management. Enablers are available for all the three phases of: Map, Build and Operationalise. Enablers are viewed through the "Knowledge Lens" discussed in Chapter 1. Some of the Enablers may be drawn from outside, even from other areas and other disciplines. The following Enablers (in alphabetical order) are to be studied and selected for utilising in Map, Build, and Operationalisation phases.

6.1. Action Taken Reviews (ATR)

Action Taken Reviews are discussions held immediately after a project or major activity. They are held in a format which may be semi-structured. These Reviews help identify "lessons" – aspects of events could be changed or improved. These Action Taken Reviews can also be conducted informally, after specific phases/milestones within a project or within a major activity.

Such frequent and immediate Action Taken Reviews on an informal basis can help create a dynamic learning process. If these Reviews are to become successful, an open organisational culture is required, along with the willingness among all the participants and stake holders to openly discuss the strengths and weaknesses. Instead of starting a "blame game", Reviews focus on discovering what exactly happened and why. Such Reviews encourage free, frank, critical discussions and also encourage innovative thinking and ideas to be implemented. They facilitate innovations by encouraging diversity of perspectives and highlighting areas and specific time-based events where a different approach could have produced a better outcome and result. Reviews have multiple roles and impact. They can act as simple housekeeping or stock taking steps and also act as occasions for critical monitoring of evaluation of the progress. They also can result in better plans based on innovative ideas to be implemented in future.

6.2. Business Process Reengineering

Knowledge Management requires integrated and coordinated approaches to work instead of the conventional compartmentalised tasks and functions. This means the organisations have to redesign their existing business processes in such a manner that an integrated approach is possible. Performance effectiveness depends critically on integrated knowledge flows.

Business Process Reengineering (BPR) changes the way organisational work is done by effective redesigning, streamlining and simplifying of the business process involved in the business functionality. Such redesign and reengineering will result in significant organisational and cultural change which may be managed by change management.

Mapping phase of business processes involves analysis of business processes – how the organisation gets its work done. It involves identifying processes for mapping, gathering information from process owners, mapping objectives, tasks, areas, flows of information and knowledge risks and success measures and also analysing gaps, inefficiencies and constraints involved in each process. By a thorough understanding of the actual process in place, it is possible to identify the gap between intended and actual processes.

From the KM perspective, focusing on business processes can provide insights into opportunities for better utilisation of knowledge for direct support of important business outcomes. Analysing how information and knowledge could best support each stage in a business process in the main outcome of Knowledge Management.

6.3. Champions and Advocates

Active and ongoing support of Champions and Advocates plays a very critical role in implementing KM initiatives and interventions within an organisation. These roles guide the building of experience and customising solutions to reflect the culture of the organisation. Thus, champions and advocates become critical success factors in implementing the cultural, organisational and technical changes required by knowledge management.

Champions and advocates with a diverse range of skills, attributes, capabilities and also passion are required to motivate and manage change. These special skills required include a good understanding of the organisation, strong personal credibility along with a strong desire to foster a change in the organisation. Thus, Champions and Advocates occupy both formal and informal leadership roles within the organisation.

6.4. Communities of Interest

Similar to champions and advocates, the Communities of Interest are critical factors for success.

These are groups of people who share knowledge and experience around a common interest. A Community of Interest is of broader scope than a Community of Practice and may have members who join simply to learn. Such communities may exist inside or even outside the organisation e.g., hobby groups, user groups, professional groups, standards groups and bench marking groups, etc.

6.5. Communities of Practice

Communities of Practice or "knowledge networks" are groups of people who develop shared expertise or interests in a specific knowledge domain.

For example, consider a government agency having multiple functional units handling a range of industry sectors. Communities of Practice have been formed across these functional units to allow professionals to share practice and expertise around the various industry sectors. Such groups or communities could usually foster relationships and bondages which would lead to collective responsibility to developing knowledge and shared understanding.

6.6. Change Management

Change Management is concerned with altering the behaviour of people. Actively managing a change intervention could be of a small scale (many such changes becoming a large change) or could be a larger change as guiding teams at multiple levels across the organisation. In all the cases, change management focuses on the social and cultural aspects of the organisation. Change Management involves several social processes including creating a committed leadership, identifying problems and offering solutions to them, empowering employees, creating a social base for change, project management and process-based team management.

Knowledge-based change interventions are used to implement behavioural shifts in the organisational culture, redefining work practices to leverage all types of knowledge and also introduce knowledge infrastructure including Intranets, online databases and Communities of Practice. The process of change itself involves mapping the parameters of change initiation, identifying the associated cultural challenges and risks and also developing an effective implementation plan. Change Management involves and calls for skill in identifying the needs and benefits of change, transferring ownership of change, developing new ideas, identifying obstacles and resistance, harnessing the organisational emotional intelligence and problem solving capabilities to influence the change.

6.7. Content Management

Content Management becomes the foundation or first step for Knowledge Management in a given organisation. It is concerned with managing organisational knowledge captured in documents and information objects through creation or acquisition, to disseminate sharing, updating use and reuse. Content can be acquired internally or externally in print, electronic or digital document forms. It may include plain data or e-mails or chats or electronic discussions, presentations, reports, policy documents, procedures, manuals, documentation, web publishing or other content forms.

Content Management and dissemination on Intranets, Extranets and Internet is to be attempted.

To summarise, Content Management comprises managing disparate flows of content and processes within an organisation, ensuring timely access to accurate and relevant knowledge, including information.

6.8. Document Management

Document Management comprises of total management of the life cycle of a document, starting from its creation, through publication, organisation, storage, retrieval, retention, and finally disposal. Document management is an activity closely associated with Record Management and Content Management. Record Management comprises management of corporate records. The documents act as evidence of business activities. Content Management comprises managing of dynamic aspects of objects. Document Management had evolved from the management of paper documents to electronic and multimedia objects that contain text, images and audio/video.

Document Management facilitates knowledge sharing by providing a single reference point for working, collaborating and connecting on the most recent versions of the document. Version control of documents is critical.

6.9. Environmental Scanning

Environmental Scanning comprises of scanning and acquisition and use of information about events, trends and relationships of the organisation with external environment. Such information and knowledge provides a clear picture of threats, opportunities and external forces of change. Such knowledge provides competitive advantage and will become input into strategic and short-term planning. This enables the organisation adapt to external environment and thereby become a learning organisation.

6.10. Auditing of Information

Conventionally and generically, Information Audit is a technique for systematically identifying, evaluating and managing organisational information resources and services. Many methodologies of Information Audit exist. While some methods concentrate on the information resources and take the form of an inventory, others consider information needs, behaviour, use and flows. Information Audit can also include the analysis of both information from within the organisation and also information flow from and to the organisation from/to its external environment.

The results of such an Audit can be descriptive, identifying gaps, duplications and inefficiencies or analytical, thereby assessing the costs of information against its value to the organisation. The strategic goal and objective of Information Audit is to establish role and scope of contribution of information to the organisational objectives and provide guidelines for effective information management. An Information Audit will also become a complement to Knowledge Audit.

6.11. Knowledge Auditing

Knowledge Audit aims at understanding the knowledge ecosystem of an organisation. It attempts at better understanding of knowledge structure, use, flow, assets and resources within an organisation and to evaluate their contribution and alignment towards the organisational objectives. Knowledge Auditing tracks the flow of tacit knowledge, expertise and skills. It also understands the knowledge culture and knowledge communities within and outside (but related to the organisation). There is no specific methodology for Knowledge Auditing. Knowledge Auditing may include needs analysis, information, communication and competency audits, using quantitative and qualitative research techniques. The results can provide the analysis of use of knowledge and practice throughout the organisation, at least within specific areas. Such an audit can provide a qualified resource and the critical evaluation of the knowledge identified can be used as an internal benchmark for the resulting interventions in Knowledge Management.

6.12. Knowledge Literacy

For implementing any intervention of Knowledge Management in an organisation, the members of the organisation are required to be literate in knowledge.

Knowledge Literacy includes the following:

(a) Skills as conversations, engaging with content (including story telling), documenting processes and mentoring,

(b) Attitudes such as openness, keenness to learn, openness to new ideas,

(c) Willingness to share knowledge without any inhibition or reservations, and

(d) Abilities to assimilate new knowledge into existing knowledge frameworks and effective participation in cross functional teams.

Any KM intervention makes demands on individuals with above attributes and qualities.

6.13. Knowledge Mapping

Knowledge-Mapping comprises mapping by visual representation of knowledge processes, sources, assets, flows, groups and knowledge barriers across the whole organisation.

While there is no standard approach to mapping of knowledge, the technique used has to be tailor-made to the knowledge environment of the organisation, focusing on people, expertise, communication, relationships, business processes, systems, products and document.

Information required for knowledge mapping can be obtained by (i) observation, (ii) contextual enquiry, (iii) interviews, (iv) process tracking, and (v) questionnaires and surveys.

Knowledge mapping brings out the knowledge ecosystem of the organisation visually. By making such visual representations, it is possible to suggest improvements and changes to the way knowledge is shared, transferred and used.

6.14. Leadership for KM

Traditionally, leadership is the human representation of the identity and core values of an organisation. In the context of knowledge, leadership strives for shared meaning, open dialogue and collaborative action. Over the time, the role of leadership is changing from managing things to coaching the organisation in managing complexity, managing its own relationships and networks (both internal and external).

In a modern connected society, the markets are very dynamic and therefore knowledge is the key driver for innovation. The real leaders in an organisation foster the knowledge creation needed to create new capabilities by helping their organisation to understand and intelligently act in the networks in which they operate.

6.15. Conclusion

In this chapter, we have surveyed the Enablers (or enabling factors) for Knowledge Management. We have presented the role of some Enablers as Action Taken Reviews, Business Process Reviews, Champions and Advocates, Communities of Interest, Communities of Practice, Change Management, Content Management, Document Management, Environmental Scanning, Auditing of Information, Knowledge Auditing, Knowledge Literacy, and Knowledge Mapping in addition to Leadership for Knowledge Management.

7

Information Technology and Knowledge Management

Information Technology (IT) and Knowledge Management (KM) have close affinity relationship. KM can be implemented by IT. Tools of IT are valuable for KM implementation, even though KM is independent.

IT is used pervasively in all organisations. The role that IT can play for Knowledge Management in an organisation is evident as a natural medium for the flow of knowledge in the organisation. Utilising and extending the existing IT infrastructure of an organisation so as to meet the KM requirements forms the first step towards the goal.

However, the negative possibilities of using IT for KM should be considered and pre-empted. Using IT for KM should not convert lively and ever growing innovative knowledge management into static information system within IT infrastructure. This eventuality should be prevented.

On the other hand, communication links, emails, chats, social networking, Wikipedia, blogs – all contribute towards better knowledge management. Databases can be developed in KM environment as repositories for best practices and Intellectual Property in terms of documents, drawings, patents, designs, etc.

"Knowledge Oriented Information Technology" is the correct theme for identifying and implementing various types of technologies and methodologies in IT domain for supporting various types of organisational knowledge during different parts of its life cycle.

7.1. KM and Workflow Processes

In a workflow, Process Knowledge is explicit, formalised knowledge about executing sequences of work activities.

Existing Process Knowledge can be enriched by letting workers externalise their understanding of new types of tasks through dynamic extension of the workflow. The benefits of coupling formalised ways of doing things with non-formal work practices obtained through direct interactions among the people can be shown and utilised. Such non-formal practices create the conditions for sharing tacit knowledge about processes. In a work group system (which is implemented in software), both these approaches can coexist and communicate, especially in a secretarial environment.

Workflow management systems can be "knowledge enabled" by moving them to a higher level in the value chain from systems for executing processes to systems for learning about processes when they are being executed. In other words, workflow management systems should come out with different levels of sophistication in the definition of a given process, just as a search engine can provide basic search or advanced search.

As the users get familiarised with the system, they shall use advanced functionality. This, in turn, may lead to the creation of new process knowledge as users may decide/design themselves new definitions for certain parts of the process or to add new sub-processes.

7.2. Organisational Memories

Organisational memories record the accumulated knowledge about the services and the products of an organisation with the purpose of supporting the continuous enhancement of knowledge intensive work practices and of alleviating the risks of "organisational amnesia" due to employees taking away their knowledge with them when they leave the organisation permanently.

It is possible to build an organisational memory in a totally unstructured manner by maintaining the physical record of all the documents and recording of all the practices of an organisation. This approach, though seemingly inexpensive, involves amassing of a lot of irrelevant information that will need to be filtered later on. The opposite approach involves an intensive initial knowledge engineering effort leading to the construction of corporate knowledge bases and expert systems. The third or middle way is to record relevant team activities through the use of hyper textual representation, linking different steps of the activities, highlighting the different options considered at each step and associating actions and decisions with roles, responsibilities and compliances of people involved. Such hyper textual representation can be created while executing the normal transaction by the knowledge workers themselves, instead of doing the same all over again by reconstruction at a later date by someone else.

Thus, process knowledge related to knowledge intensive problem solving and decision-making activities gets recorded. In this manner, we may get a specific "view point" of knowledge, as opined by the concerned knowledge workers (user).

Multiple views of such kind may require reconciliation at a later stage.

7.3. Information Filtering

Information filtering has become crucial type of IT support for knowledge workers who are faced with ever increasing volumes of information from sources internal to the organisation and also from external sources as the world wide web.

Information filtering can be done in many ways. One such mechanism is to set up filters based on "interests" of individuals to measure the relevance of information being processed. The profile of the individual giving his/her "interests" can be utilised for filtering purposes. Simple natural language conditions or queries can be converted into weighted graphs that capture the semantic content of the query (with respect to the given profile). These graphs can be utilised for filtering.

User Profiling can also be combined with conventional information retrieval systems. Adaptive information filtering capabilities can be implemented with greater accuracy than regular methods.

A part of the "workflow" related to a specific search of information can be automated through an intelligent agent system that leverages memory-based reasoning techniques to select relevant information sources and make suggestions for such actions as storing returned documents into appropriate folders, deleting, printing, etc. These agents may learn and time their own behaviours by direct observation of user's behaviours.

7.4. Software Process Improvement using Knowledge Management

While knowledge and information are closely related to each other, Nonaka and Takenchi showed how knowledge can be externalised into information. Therefore, both knowledge and information have to be managed. Thus, IM (Information Management) and KM (Knowledge Management) are closely related, i.e., KM has to cover Information Management (IM). After all, KM is a Business Process Reengineering (BPR) activity to improve current processes with respect to better utilisation (creation and sharing) of knowledge. Accordingly, the experiences from BPR and SPI (Softwre Process Integration) can be applied to KM.

7.4.1. Knowledge Management in Virtual Software Corporation (VSC)

With the Internet becoming ubiquitous, as a general trend, it is possible to have virtual corporations performing close cooperative interactions between a number of organisations. In software business, such corporations are called Virtual Software Corporations (VSCs). Such organisations link dynamically their processes to achieve their business goals. The potential synergy effects are economics of scale and scope, enforced market functions and quality improvements, thus bringing together the best of the two worlds – markets and hierarchies – at least in some situations.

Ultimately, all these activities are identifiable as Software Engineering which is highly knowledge-intensive task requiring the mediation of knowledge, i.e., Knowledge Management (KM).

We may assume that KM is a management tool for future software development. The KM Process Model enables a detailed understanding of the processes needed to be performed within KM and can thereby assist in analysing, planning and conducting KM for software engineering. The problems of Virtual Software Corporations (VSCs) addressed include knowledge mediation which indicates that a KM-based approach to VSC may be a solution to these problems. KM process model is theoretically applicable to Virtual Software Corporations (VSCs) as given below:

As stated by Nonaka, while knowledge is created in the minds of people only, it can be still transferred to others in several ways as: Socialisation (tacit to tacit), Externalisation (tacit to explicit), Combination (explicit to explicit) and Internalisation (explicit to tacit).

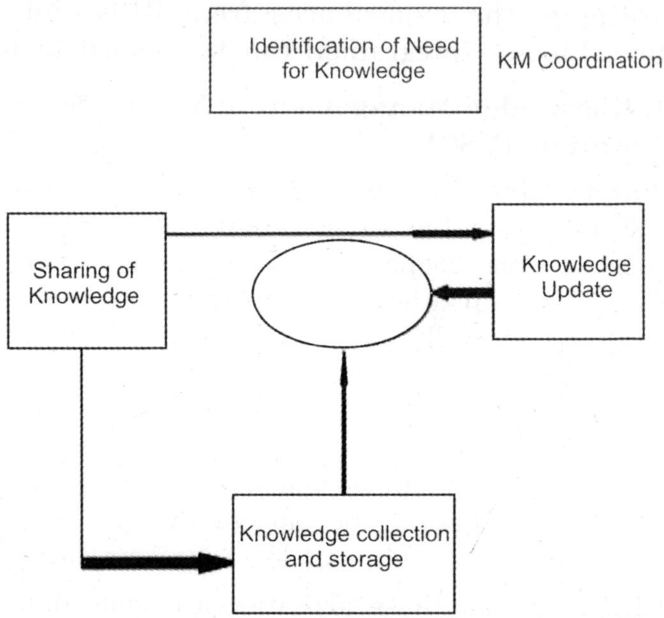

Fig. 7.1: KM Process Model and Primer Improvement Model.

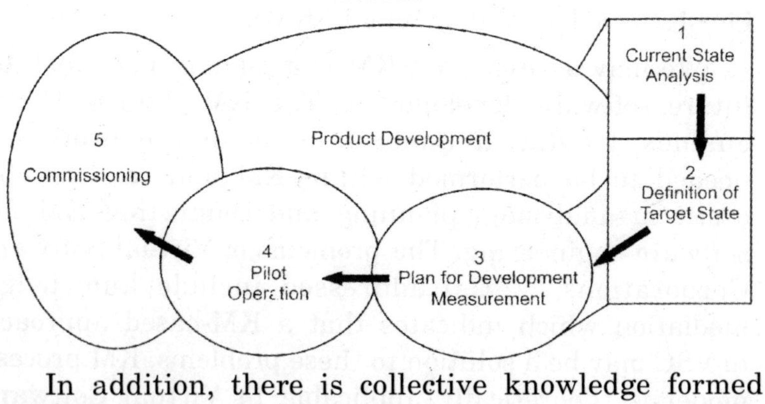

In addition, there is collective knowledge formed by different groups of people and the way (processes) they work together (organisational knowledge). The Fig. 1 above introduces KM process model and illustrates primer improvement model.

The basic processes of KM indicated in Fig. 1 above are being described below:

KM Coordination: This is implemented according to the principles of Primer Model used for guiding and controlling improvement initiatives. The current status (of software) is analysed and a target state is set, which is defined based on the scope of the improvement project. In the analysis phase knowledge processes, cultural environment and technical means related to software engineering processes, (e.g., software reuse processes) are subject to analysis. Based on the problems so found and the needs, the goals for improvement and better practices are defined. During pilot operation and commissioning, improved KM and Software Engineering practices are monitored by analysing the collected metrics. Primer process build up an improvement cycle (Analyse – Define – Plan – Effect) to address the need to take an incremental approach (starting with pilots, ending up with comprehensive systems) and to be able to adopt to changing environments. The following "Learning" Process is performed:

(i) **Identification of Need for Knowledge:** Before the existing knowledge can be used/ reused, the need for knowledge has to be identified and the requirements for that desired knowledge have to be determined. Organisational culture plays an important role in such identification, as also technology application for the activities involved therein.

(ii) **Sharing of Existing Knowledge:** If the required knowledge is already present, it needs to be shared. For this, the corresponding knowledge has to be searched for amongst knowledgeable people or explicit knowledge has to be found. Sharing can be made to happen either by "Knowledge Pull" (people search for knowledge) or "Knowledge Push" (people are provided with knowledge they are known to be needing). Knowledge can further be shared outside the organisation (Knowledge Brokering). A major enabler for sharing knowledge will be the society and cultural environment, which is addressed in "KM coordination". After supporting culture is built, supporting technological assistance should be introduced.

(iii) **Creation of new Knowledge:** If the identified "Need for Knowledge" is not available, it has to be created in different ways: Cycles of convergent and divergent thinking are performed in creating innovations. If knowledge is taken from external sources, it has to be recreated in conjunction with the existing knowledge to achieve adoption to the actual environment. Therefore knowledge coming from outside will go into knowledge creation stage and not directly to utilisation (sharing or storage).

(iv) **Knowledge Collection and Storage:** New Knowledge is not only created by demand, but also by innovations during the standard work processes and procedures, without explicit intention (accidental discovery or innovation and invention). Whenever knowledge is created, it needs to be identified, and then evaluated to determine how it can be stored, shared or distributed via the process of "Sharing of existing Knowledge". Storage and mediation can be performed by externalisation to explicit knowledge – this process has to be covering the media, codification, generation of metadata for searching, etc.

(v) **Knowledge Update:** Knowledge changes with changing environments as it is context- specific. Threfore, it has to be kept up-to-date, otherwise the whole KM system is endangered. Thus, changes need to be identified and analysed from the point of view of their impact on existing knowledge. Appropriate updates at appropriate cycles as per the needs has to be undertaken. In a Virtual Software Configuration (VSC), a KM system has to address the following issues:

- Building an entry level trust between all potential partners.
- Managing the pool of potential partners and assisting them in getting the right combination of partners for specific purposes.
- Building a required minimum level of trust between partners performing a project together.
- Providing the means for mediating knowledge between the cooperating partners in a project (collecting, storing, finding and transferring) according to the performed tasks.

7.4.2. Methodology for KM Implementation in Virtual Software Corporations (VSCs)

In the following section, the methodology is shown on how to apply the KM Process Model for both the dimensions, i.e., VSC Dimension (connecting all possible partners) and VSC Project Dimension (connecting a number of partners building a concrete goal-oriented VSC).

(a) VSC Dimension – VSC has to be established as a common basis for all potential partners (partner pool). Standards may be used for this. Processes for forming projects and general information and knowledge about VSCs needs to be shared with all, using a web site providing all possible information such as a list of available projects and their status, glossary of terms, general description on how to cooperate in the Projects, etc. Regular meetings between all partners are desirable to exchange information and build a general level of trust. Occasional meetings, conferences, workshops, exhibitions, etc., could be arranged. Success stories (codified knowledge) can be disseminated for motivation.

(b) VSC – Project Dimension – Within a single project, the KM requirements are met in this phase. All partners in a project are connected by the outgoing knowledge brokering processes ("knowledge sharing") to the incoming knowledge acquisition processes ("knowledge creation"). This is a representation of the network that the partners build on the knowledge level to create and share knowledge. After completion of the Project, their knowledge will be distributed into first phase above, i.e., VSC Dimension.

7.4.3. KM Process Model Utilisation in a Virtual Software Corporation (VSC)

Firstly, the analysis has to be performed to identify the existing knowledge with the potential partners. After this, make sure that "Knowledge Map" so prepared is available to all partners. A website-based presentation could be prepared. The management of possible projects and means for finding partners with suitable knowledge to put up a team also could be realised in this manner. Meetings to create trust can be arranged – knowledge about how to build and manage teams in a VSC can be provided. By deploying these initial processes, the KM system is started. Concrete projects in a VSC could utilise different levels of Processes. Regular meetings could be organised for extending level of trust and exchange of knowledge. Methods on how to improve communication by utilising technology and addressing security issues, how to establish a common workspace using video conferencing, etc., can be planned and executed. Project experiences can be shared extensively and intensively among the members of partner pool. Codification of processes and project level knowledge can be done.

7.5. Knowledge Management (KM) and Information Security Management (ISM) (KM and ISM)

Knowledge Management and Information Security Management have a lot of similarities. Knowledge Management is defined as "the capability by which communities capture knowledge that is crucial to their success, constantly improve it, and make it available in the most cost-effective manner to those who need it" (Birkenkrahe 2002). Also, "KM deals with the process of creating value from an organisation's intangible assets" (Lebounty 1999) and it comprises "conceptualisation, review, consolidation and action phases of creating, securing, combining, coordinating and retrieving knowledge".

Information Security on the other hand, is usually described as "preservation of confidentiality", integrity and availability of information along with other properties as "authenticity, accountability, non-repudiation and reliability" (ISO/IEC 20035).

Among various definitional terms used for Information Security, "Confidentiality", "Integrity" and "availability of information" can be identified to be central to Information Security. Accordingly, Information Security Management (ISM) can be defined as the management of activities being aimed at the confidentiality, integrity and availability of organisational internal information.

In this section, we shall demonstrate multiple similarities between KM and ISM.

7.5.1. Similarities between KM and ISM

Both KM and ISM are rated high in the importance rating of information within the organisation. Both KM and ISM are usually handled by the Information

Technology (IT) Department and Chief Information Officer (CIO) of the organisation. They both share certain common characteristics which support the possibility of translating established solutions from one area to the other.

7.5.2. Dependence on People

In both the domains of Knowledge Management and Information Security Management, the dependence on people is critical. In KM, people have to share their individual knowledge, both tacit and explicit, with others to form and establish a comprehensive body of knowledge which can be profitably used all over the organisation. That knowledge will be capitalised by others in the organisation.

In the case of Information Security, the same thing is true. "People are cornerstones of Information Security". To make Information Security work, people have to behave in a secure manner, should not circumvent the existing security mechanisms, and should develop a sense of making right decisions in case of unforeseen events.

7.5.3. Public Good Production

"Public goods" are defined as those outputs produced whose production will not result in reduction of anything else (e.g., knowledge). In Knowledge Management, production of knowledge is the output and it will not result in reduction of anything else, i.e., non-rivalry. KM is executed to create and sustain a body of knowledge which can be used all over the organisation to generate profit. Making use of knowledge so generated will result in higher working efficiency. Exclusive use of knowledge is not recommended. Inclusion for knowledge usage is always for the larger good of the organisation.

The principle of non-rivalry will result from the

non-physical nature of knowledge. As information, knowledge also can be used after its production, repeatedly at minimal or at zero cost leading to non-security. Usage of knowledge is not restricted to one or some members (unless it is strictly confidential).

The above statements are applicable to Information Security also. Once a solution of enhancing Information Security is developed and established, there is no case of rivalry in its usage. Information Security does not decrease for an individual member if it is used by more people. Non-exclusion is also present for information security. With Information Security being fundamental and non-rival requirement for smooth operation of an organisation, it would not make any sense in excluding any member from taking its advantage. The fact of the matter is that the opposite is more true. If Information Security facilities are not availed by some sections of the organisation, then the vulnerability of the organisation is enhanced.

To summarise, both KM and IS share a second similarity, i.e., being aimed at the production of organisation internal pubic goods.

7.5.4. Exclusively Usable Knowledge

KM aims at making available all knowledge in an organisation to all relevant members of the organisation. Individual knowledge has to be divulged across the entire organisation so as to increase the internal knowledge of the organisation, which in turn results in increasing the profitab·lity of the organisation. Such higher or enhanced internal knowledge level of an organisation reflects on its competence and competitiveness by providing an edge over the other organisations who may not exactly compare or equalise their internal knowledge levels. In other words, knowledge that can be used by all the members of the organisation promises higher profit than individual knowledge and knowledge that remains secret from the competitors promises higher profits than knowledge that is publicly available. KM, therefore, is aimed at expanding the body of exclusively usable knowledge.

In the context of Information Security domain, confidentiality, integrity and availability of information are the main classical goals of Information Security. By applying these goals to the body of exclusively usable knowledge, it will be clear that Information Security is not aimed exactly at increasing the internal knowledge level, but protecting the existing information and knowledge from being lost or preventing its decrease. Confidentiality decreases the risk of business secrets getting known by rivals, and therefore, assure exclusiveness: integrity prevents knowledge from being manipulated and availability is targeted against cases of existing knowledge not being usable for the members of the organisation.

Therefore, information security management is similar to knowledge management, being aimed at having a positive effect on the body of exclusively usable knowledge.

7.6. Organisational Challenge

Finally, as a similarity, both KM and ISM share the challenges of optimisation. In case of Information Security, even though giving normally positive payoff, there will be a threshold value beyond which security implementation may result in negative payoff.

Two main reasons for a negative payoff could be:

With every investment towards information security, the existing balance risks decrease and become more costly to decrease further. At some state, a point is reached where the expected loss from a risk not being eliminated is lower than the cost of eliminating it. Secondly, if there is too much security in working place, the working itself gets less efficient due to a growing number of restrictions and constraints, which may result in substantial loss of profit which may have been avoided otherwise. This may result in "diminishing returns". Therefore, the organisation has to find the optimal level of security where the marginal benefits of an additional counter measure equals its marginal costs.

For KM, the optimisation challenge is similar. Up to a certain point, this refurbishment of existing knowledge and creation of new knowledge may result in an overall benefit to the organisation, exceeding the costs that have to be borne due to loss of productive working time (for implementing KM).

Just as in the case of Information Security, there will always be a point where the marginal benefits of additional knowledge management efforts is lower than the resulting marginal cost. In both KM and ISM, the challenge of optimisation is finding the point from where additional efforts will start becoming counter-productive.

To summarise, four major similarities between the areas of corporate information security management and knowledge management are:

1. The strong involvement of and dependency on people,
2. The aim of producing an internal public good for the organisation,
3. A positive effect on the exclusively usable knowledge, and
4. Underlying problem of optimisation of finding the optimal level from where the additional costs and inefficiencies outreach additional benefits.

7.7. Conclusion

In this chapter, we have surveyed the common features of KM and IT in the context of workflows, processes and memories of the organisation, and also information filtering. We have also presented the models for application of KM into Virtual Software Corporation (VSC), both in general level and project specific levels. We have also presented a comparative analysis of similarities between KM and ISM.

Reference

1. "Using KM in software process improvement – the creation of KM process model" by Timokuca, Seija Komisirvio, VIT Electronics, Kaitavalya, 1, PL 1100, 90571, Onlu, Finland Timkokuzca, Saija Komi – Sirvio @ vtf.fi).

8

Knowledge Transfer

Knowledge Management is considered to be a major focus area in knowledge and learning industry, especially the IT or software industry in the fast growing competitive world. Everyone among the developers and also organisations are making attempts at reducing cost and time for the decision-making process with the use of knowledge. This sector captures knowledge (tacit and explicit) of the past for using in problem solving in future. Knowledge workers — as software developers — develop and ascertain various aspects regarding the technological process resulting in valuable output. The KM based development and sharing helps the organisation to develop group dynamics and group activity in a systematic way giving the end product. The transfer and management of knowledge in an organisation should be emphasised in an organisation to create competitive advantage. The use of knowledge from various levels and transfer from one level to another should be developed. Generations to generations knowledge transfer should take place. Accumulated Enterprise knowledge is a new type of knowledge that can be retrieved by a generation employees from time to time.

8.1. Successive Knowledge Transfer (KT)

All knowledge workers desire for transfer of

knowledge to successive groups of employees in a form which reduces time and cost.

Knowledge Transfer (KT) and its management takes time and is also expensive. Upon utilisation, the cost reduces and thus becomes advantageous. By doing so, the organisation, especially knowledge industry, gets maximum benefits during the regular problem-solving and decision-making processes.

An organisation critically depends on various factors and resources among which human resource is the most critical, especially in knowledge industry. Human resource in an organisation is capable of handling and maintaining the idea of an instant and wise decision based on knowledge and other factors like environment. Value is represented by the use of expensive Knowledge Management Systems (KMSs). In software sector, the knowledge worker develops and ascertains various aspects about the technological process, resulting in valuable output. Software development (both for applications and products) is a process in which group dynamics and group activity occur in a systematic way, delivering the end product. If the phases get disturbed in between, the output cannot be delivered and therefore, the overall effort input gets wasted.

The transfer of knowledge or code from one member to another helps the organisation earn revenue and gain advantages. Therefore, in a knowledge intensive environment, knowledge creation as the source of sustainable competitive advantage has become widespread among practitioners as well as researchers. During the process of each decision, each development and each activity are to be captured and stored to be used by the subordinates and new employees subsequently.

In the case of collaborations between two different organisations, strategic alliances have to be signed to identify and develop success formula by sharing knowledge as a major component of collaborations in planning. Sharing of knowledge can also be represented as Knowledge Transfer (KT), from one organisation to another, for mutual benefit. Due emphasis on KT and management will help the organisation to develop its programmes in large. The knowledge success factor and knowledge management cycle will help the organisation to achieve competitive advantage.[1] Organisations can create knowledge, store, transfer, and manage environments by using various methods like incentives to the employees, using different approaches which help the employees to spread knowledge, develop regular appraisal techniques to the level of KT.

8.2. Knowledge Sources

What are various sources of knowledge? The following are some of the sources of knowledge:

1. Text documents
   (a) Notes
   (b) Books
   (c) Reports
   (d) Files
   (e) Minutes of the Meetings
   (f) Legislations
   (g) Records of Proceedings
2. Comments
   (a) Comments by Management
   (b) Comments by Experts
3. Innovation of Processes
   (a) Employee innovations of Processes

Knowledge can be accessed by individuals from various sources of data in the organisation (as libraries, record rooms, etc). The knowledge so accessed can be filtered to create "understanding", and "wisdom", later.

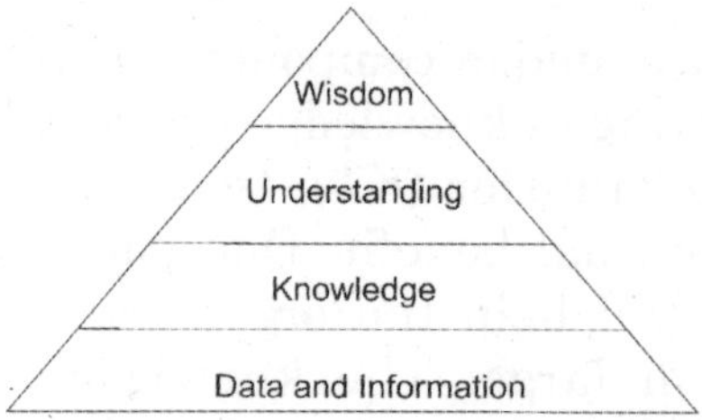

Fig. 8.1: Hierarchy of Knowledge Transfer (KT), Dissemination, Sharing, Learning, Problem-Solving, Decision-Making and Gaining Knowledge.

Wisdom comprises the very essence and epitome of essence of knowledge, acquired by a long period of thorough understanding and application of knowledge.

8.3. Knowledge Development Stages and Cycles

Fig. 8.2 below represented Knowledge Development Stages and Cycles.

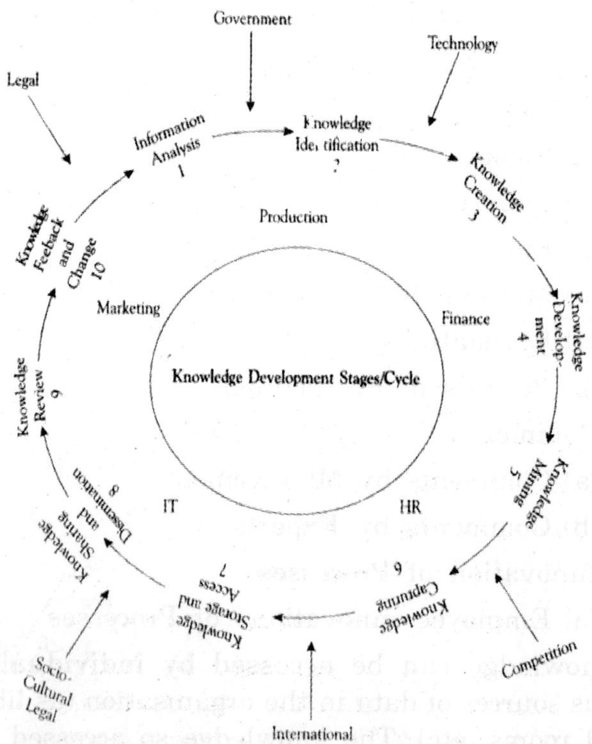

Fig. 8.2: Knowledge Development Stages and Cycles.

- **Information/Data Analysis:** Before starting the activities related to knowledge development in the organisation, one should look after the data/ information sources and usage of the material in the organisation. Sources of information refer to various questions like: Why it is collected? Who? When? How it can be used in a better way? Answering these questions may be termed as information auditing.
- **Knowledge Identification:** Information auditing should be capable of identifying and separating relevant set of instructions and processes, which can act as knowledge or be used as a base to solve the organisation problem. The major aspect of the stage is to define valuable knowledge, to make decision, so that it can be used to save cost and time.
- **Knowledge Creation/Development:** Identification of the knowledge can be done in a mixed form which may sometimes mismatch with others. Segregation and arranging a set of system can be readily used for solving the knowledge needs of the organisation. It also looks upon various areas and functions of business for the development of tools, for decision-making process.
- **Knowledge Mining and Filtering:** The organisation uses previous knowledge for its decision-making and problem-solving process. Based on the situation and forces acting internally and externally, newer information can be used as knowledge for the business purpose. The knowledge bank can also be used again and filtered for extracting newer ideas and skills. Newer knowledge can also be developed according to the situation of the organisation.
- **Knowledge Capturing:** Changing environment and its forces differ from organisation to

organisation and function to function. The newer skills, information, expertise should be captured and developed to improve the processes. The functional changes based on the environmental forces should be captured in the form of knowledge for long-run development.

- **Knowledge Storage and Access:** Technology plays a crucial role in the process of knowledge storage and access. Information Technology helps in data storage and retrieval process. Each decision-making process should be recorded and stored in such a form, which can be easily accessed by the subordinates for solving problem and making decision. The tacit knowledge which is difficult to store, should be framed by individual knowledge worker.
- **Knowledge Storing and Dissemination:** Knowledge storage should be accessible in shareable mode. The different functional units of the organisation should have the privilege to share and to create new ideas and disseminate for innovation process. Knowledge sharing can be done within different organisations, operating under different areas. It can be used to analyse the external forces like government, changing policy and the resulting effect on the organisation. Knowledge sharing can also be used for solving problems from different external forces like economic depression, environmental protection, poverty reduction, pollution control, and so on.
- **Knowledge Review, Transfer and Addition:** Knowledge can be reviewed and added after different opinions from organisation community. Sharing KT can be possible inside and outside the organisation. It needs organisation and scanning to anticipate knowledge needs. It will

be possible by involving stakeholders in knowledge review and transferring processes.

- **Knowledge Feedback and Change Agents:** The stakeholders after reviewing the existing knowledge give feedback whether the knowledge leads to better decision-making and higher productivity and performance. The feedback will act as change agents and give information to analyse stage 1 which will follow knowledge development cycle.

8.4 External and Internal Factors Affecting Knowledge Development Cycle

The organisation is surrounded by both internal and external factors which affect the organisation and functions and working. The knowledge-managed organisation extracts information and knowledge from both internal and external environment. The internal environment comprises production, marketing, human capital, technology, warehousing, etc. The external factors comprising economic conditions, technology, competition, socio-cultural environment and changing forces are analysed by the organisation which forms a sort of knowledge guiding the organisation to develop new strategies. The organisation can follow alternatives or same strategies in the near future for the problems arisen in the environment. Various forces acting against organisation can be taken into consideration as information and can be further transformed into knowledge. Subsequent detailed information re-analysed under knowledge development cycle can be used for problem-solving and decision- making process.

8.5 Knowledge Transfer

The major focus in this chapter is to engage the knowledge enterprises to transfer knowledge which is difficult in case of implicit knowledge. Nonaka and Takeuchi (1995) propose four knowledge processes that build on the distinctions between tacit and explicit knowledge: socialisation, internalisation, combination and externalisation. The transference of knowledge from an old and experienced employee to new and inexperienced, developing subordinated under various stages, process the information into knowledge by analysing, identifying, creating, capturing, storing and sharing among different functional groups.

Knowledge in an organisation exists at different levels. It includes:

(a) Enterprise level

(b) Employees level

(a) Enterprise level: It consists of wider and system-based knowledge which includes records of all the regular activities and operational processes happening in an institution. This explicit form of knowledge can be retrieved by the new employees at different levels, time and functional situations. It includes duties, responsibilities, procedure functions and operational areas and hierarchal level. The enterprises can store these data and information in any form which can be stored and disseminated among all employees and accessed at any point of time for learning and decision-making.

(b) Employees level: Based on the available knowledge at enterprise level, employees use the understanding based on the functional specific area. The tacit form of knowledge differs from employee to employee and function to function. This difference is due to the skills, abilities and experience gained by the employee. The use of individual characteristics for the achievement of the organisation's objective and decision-making at institutional level should be captured and utilised. The process of capturing individual knowledge is difficult as it is shaded and also because sometimes decision-making is a group effort where every group member plays a vital role.

For exmple, development of software product is done by a group where each individual puts his understanding and knowledge to achieve the output.

The synergy between the individual, group and enterprises should be developed to form the process of KT and management. The creation of such combination will create the knowledge bank or pool from which retrieval can be possible during the execution of various business processes.

The transfer of knowledge in both enterprises and individual levels, can be formed as a knowledge bank which can be accessed by new and subordinate employees. Fig. 8.3 represents knowledge bank.

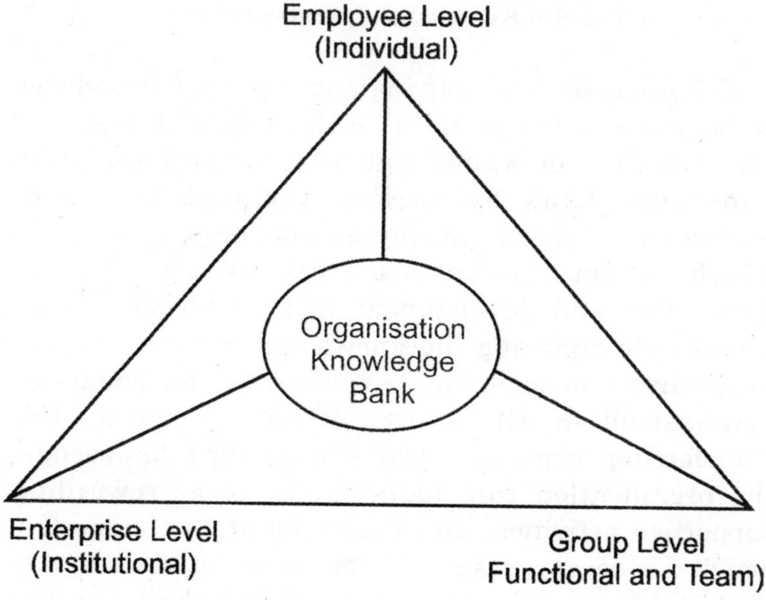

Fig. 8.3: Creation of Knowledge Bank and its Components.

The transfer of knowledge can be possible within and outside functional or departmental level. Fig. 8.4 represents knowledge sharing and transferring processes.

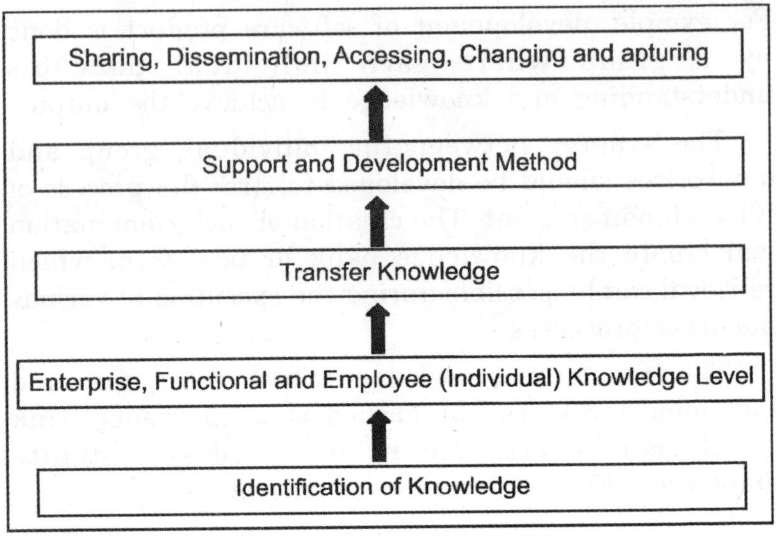

Fig. 8.4: Knowledge Transfer Levels.

KT starts from identifying and capturing knowledge at enterprises, functional as well as individual levels. The transfer of knowledge can be possible from knowledge bank by various components. These components refer to employees and enterprise group which reflect human resources as key aspects. Supportive and development method of KT can be adopted for capturing the knowledge at various levels. Supportive functions like, technology for KT should be emphasised in all aspects of an enterprise. For transferring, capturing and storing tacit knowledge, the organisation can adopt incentive or rewarding supportive activities. The main aim of the supportive activity is to encourage KT and store in such a way that it can be shared and used by others for the achievement of organisational objectives. Rewarding employees to actively participate in KT activity should be the main motive of the organisation.

The knowledge transformation and development stages (Fig. 8.2) will help the organisation to transform information into knowledge and promote understanding at each level. The transfer level starts from identification of information and knowledge which is done extensively at enterprises, employee and individual level. The creation and development of knowledge is done at each of these levels from where the knowledge is captured and analysed for its usefulness. Meanwhile, various environmental factors like competition, legal, political, government, etc., act as external factors and internally, marketing, production and other factors provide affecting factors. Supportive and development method (Fig. 8.4) and tools will help the organisation to capture and store the knowledge appropriately. This overall development model will help the organisation to transfer knowledge and disseminate, share, access, etc., for attaining organisational objectives.

KT can be done by various methods like interview, storytelling, essay writing, etc. The leaders must encourage and participate in informal exchange, discussions, supply of resources, and rewarding for successful KT. The successful KT should give productivity, achieve better performance and add value to decision-making process. The process of KT should be followed to ensure measurement of the output and capability of using better method of learning and sharing.

8.6 Knowledge Transfer (KT) Methods

KT methods represented in this paper can be used in separate and in combination based on the need and system. KT method includes:

(a) Induction method

(b) Counselling method

(c) Employees rotation method

(d) Training and development method

(e) Group learning method

(a) Induction method: This method can be best used for transferring the explicit and enterprise knowledge to the newly recruited employees. Induction method acquaints the new employee with enterprise objectives, goals, mission, hierarchical structure, employment conditions, etc. Induction can also be used separately by different functional or departmental levels to transfer specific knowledge to an individual or employee (e.g., employee specification, responsibility, work area and environment, expected outcomes, benefits, compensation, incremental aspects, conduct, role, etc.). The former can be done on a group basis and transfer of knowledge can be from one to many and/or many to many. The latter can be achieved for many to one or one to one in an organisation setup. Fig. 8.5 shows the difference between both.

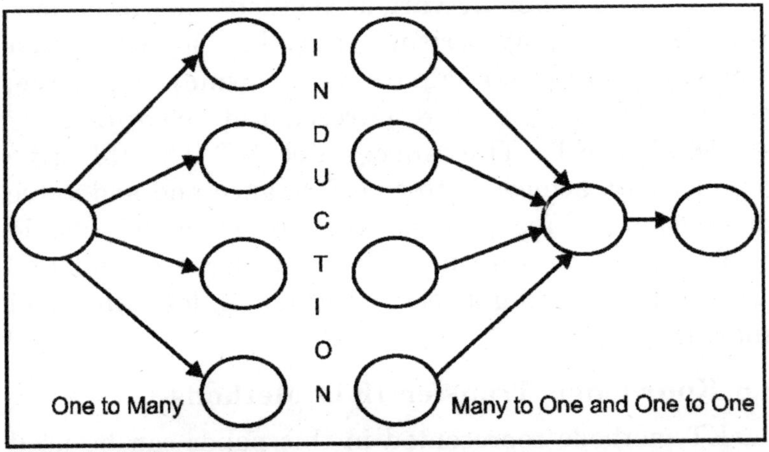

Fig. 8.5: Knowledge Transfer Through Induction.

Induction method in an organisation is one of the best methods for capturing the explicit and enterprises knowledge, to the newly recruited employee. The transfer of the explicit knowledge includes strategies, method of working, development of skill, organisational environmental conditions, etc., which differs from organisation to organisation. The newly employed member may or may not have full idea and knowledge about the organisation. These methods will provide the employee with adequate knowledge about the organisation for his/her working. It includes knowledge about mission, vision, goals and objectives, etc. The capturing of the explicit knowledge can be possible in the form of presentations or recording the program in various forms.

Objective of Induction Method

The major objective of the induction method is to transfer knowledge which is likely to be kept in mind for a new employee and make adjustment to his/her job and the organisation. The method helps the employee to adapt to an organisational culture and environment. The major objectives served for the group and the employee are represented in Table 8.1.

Table 8.1: Objectives for the Group and the Employee

Group and Employee (Both	Employee
Understanding organisation's objectives, mission, policies, procedures, etc.	Functional and positional responsibility
Understanding group dynamics	Duties, responsibilities and roles
Group knowledge sharing	Health and safety
Duties and position	Service, Incentives, benefits, etc.
Association	Professional service

Induction method of KT can also be provided to all its stakeholders like customers, suppliers, distributors, agents and employees by its webpage with different links to the organisation's functions and resources. It provides knowledge about various aspects like products and services, availability, activities, and so on. It is not only restricted to the internal people but also to the external public.

(b) Counselling Method: The method of KT is capable of giving immediate result to both explicit and tacit knowledge within the employees of the organisation. The process of counselling is intended to provide transfer of knowledge form one generation to another cluster form. This mechanism will help the organisation to create group dynamics and transfer of knowledge within shorter duration of time. The organisation attaches a new employee to his senior for professional development which helps the organisation to transfer explicit and tacit knowledge. The process of counselling can be recorded and stored during the time period. The major objective of the method is to develop group dynamics, build professional equality, enhance communication among different levels and promote continuous learning, improve performance and productivity at the initial phases of the employee, improve decision-making by transfer of skills, ability and experience.

The counselling method can be adopted in a transparent cultural diversity in the form of an extensive communication from senior level to junior level. The method has the potential to transmit expertise, extend support to senior level and develop the human resources to create high potential employee as an advantage to the organisation. The counselling method is used by various organisations to transfer the tacit knowledge from the senior level to the junior level of employees. The counselling method is also called mentoring process. The process can be captured by various methods like, storytelling in which the junior employee can explain his/her experience in the form of a story which they learn or gain during the process. This can be recorded as transforming tacit knowledge into explicit one. The new employee can gain knowledge of decision-making, problem-solving, etc., through this process. The essentials (knowledge) of decision-making and problem-solving can be gained by the counsellor or mentor to whom they are assigned. This indicates the KT process.

During the process of regular advancement of the senior and junior level employee, the organisation develops additional human resource capital, transforming new employee to be productive and expert in his/her field. Most of the organisations adopt counselling method at the initial phases where the new employee is counselled by different people (many to one) and functional area to have overall development and is then attached to his specialised area supervisor to acquire his/her functional expertise (one to one). The follow-up evaluation is done for regular reporting to the organisation regarding performance, productivity, learning, by which the organisation estimates the amount of KT within the process with minimal cost and efforts. The organisation can adopt the method for long duration of time, based on cost.

(c) Employee Rotation Method: The employee within the organisation is transferred for shorter duration from one department/functional area to another, to get exposure to functional knowledge of the organisation. The definite program is developed for the specific number of days/months. Normally, the organisation selects particular number of employees for particular program without disturbing regular program. These programs are conducted with high level of input (knowledge) given to the participant in shorter duration. The major objective of the method is to improve efficiency and effectiveness by the transfer of knowledge in a way that allows the employee to move up in the hierarchy and includes:

- Improving professional and decision-making skills by providing exposure to different functional units for the upward movement.
- Improving relationship among different staff members who are correlated to each other for a particular set of activities.
- Expanding overall outlook and knowledge of the employee in a broad way and at organisational level helping the employee to understand and develop potential for higher position.

The employee rotation method is based on the human resources available within the organisation. Limited amount of cost will be incurred for adoption of this method. The major stress is to effectively transfer understanding and knowledge assessing the capability and skills for upward mobility of employee in an organisational hierarchy.

(d) Training and Development Method: The traditional method of KT includes enhancing skills, professional ability, knowledge and learning, productivity, motivation, adjusting to the work environment and improving overall performance of the employee. The method is usually adopted at different stages, levels and cost. The major objective is to develop skills and improve performance by retaining the employees and achieving higher level of output.

The organisation allocates budgets and initiates training and development on a regular basis, assessing each employee's performance and investing time and cost for continuous, structured and specific program. The method serves for:

- Promoting employee to achieve higher performance,
- Developing and supporting new employees to adjust in organisation environment and developing relationship among other employees,

- Enhancing efficiency and effectiveness,
- Improving productivity and quality, and
- Acquainting employees with new strategies, policies and procedures.

Training method is not only useful for improving performance but also acts as a KT method in which the trainee will undergo the process of doing things under the guidance of the experienced and knowledgeable trainer. The trainer will develop the trainee by transferring the knowledge during the process, which the trainee applies to achieve or improve the performance. For example, if the trainee from marketing sales department will be assigned to the trainer from marketing packaging and distribution area, the trainer will develop and add knowledge of the packaging and distribution, i.e., the transfer of knowledge through training.

The organisation can achieve a number of advantages by training and development method of KT like:

- Easy knowledge transfer,
- Retain employees who are skilled and trained,
- Reduce employees turn over,
- Employee's motivation and satisfaction,
- Improve quality of work, and
- Adopt newer techniques and processes.

(e) Group Learning Method: The group learning method of KT can be widely used in an organisation at different levels. It can be informal as well as formal method of learning. The organisation can develop a program each working week among functional group/ teams, branch and even organisational level for group learning. The KT is possible with a group of people who come together to transfer knowledge with different experience and share learning. During the process, high

level executive will analyse the problem and discuss the same which develops common understanding and promote KT among the employees. The insight on various issues and practices will exceptionally transfer knowledge and achieve group learning.

During the process, implicit knowledge can be easily transferred and can be disseminated to a larger group of employees at the same time. The major advantages of the group learning method includes: within the organisation and functional area it will review performance standards, sustain strength and relation within the employees and group can review lessons learnt during last decision-making and problem-handling. It will lead to group dynamics and learning within organisation. It will also develop team motivation and strive for better result formally and sometimes informally. The group learning method helps informal and small community to learn and acquire knowledge, aligning with the organisation's goals and objectives.

The organisation should structure the group learning method by identifying strong, committed, experienced professional within the organisation as a leader, to drive the group in reaching particular knowledge gaining result. Each knowledge transmission and sharing should be recorded and disseminated across the organisation. The technology will provide support for knowledge sharing, capturing and dissemination. The effective KT will help the organisation for creating awareness in the organisation regarding the knowledge sharing. The process of group learning establishes "trust" and creates "transparency" within the organisation and explores new opportunities to review the old lesson learning, reduces error and instils potential into new techniques and process.

The method helps the organisation to reduce cost and time for disseminating knowledge among employees as knowledge base is shared captured and created at the same time. Organising group learning will help the working community to build knowledge in less time and cost and will induce a strong commitment among employees as a team.

Knowledge Sharing Culture in an Organisation

Knowledge sharing culture in an organisation can be developed in various forms based on the availability of resources. The methods discussed above like training method, group learning, employees rotation, counselling method are successful when there is some incentive involved behind the activity to the employees. Most of the organisations have the incentive method for the purpose of conducting the activities. Other methods include:

- *Shared Development:* Encourages to develop shared understanding on various issues in an organisation. The individual efforts should be transferred and encouraged in a group/team efforts which develop shared knowledge. The shared development with the employee in relation to mission, target performance, productivity, organisational development and success should be encouraged.
- *Focus on Knowledge Development Cycle:* The managers should be efficient enough to practice the knowledge development cycle regularly as it identifies information and uses that information to get knowledge, giving a better understanding and problem solving approach. Knowledge development cycle will act as a transformation tool.
- *Knowledge Supportive Environment:* Encouraging knowledge supportive environment within the organisation will improve the success. The information generated in any functional area

should be arranged and recorded, to be transmitted in knowledge development cycle, which provides support for the problem solving.

- *Knowledge Flow:* The organisation should practice the frequent flow of knowledge at different levels in proper quality and quantity. The flow of knowledge should be certain and should be organised, used and widely leveraged.

References

1. Mathur, V. (2007), Business Review, Vol. 1, No. 1.
2. "The Critical Knowledge Transfer in an Organisation: Approaches" by Viju Mathew and Mary Kavitha. ICFAIJ of KM, Vol. VI, No. 4, July, 2008.

9

Distributed Knowledge Management Systems (DKMS) for Internet Age

The Internet age is characterised by distributed objects spread over the Internet. Accordingly, architecture of Distributed Knowledge Management Systems based on distributed objects became important.

9.1. Distributed/Object Oriented Datawarehouse/ Distributed Knowledge Management System

In the Internet scenario, data warehousing development comprises evolutionary development of distributed objects. The concept of data warehousing to describe the activity of enterprise-wise distributed processing leads to the concept of "Distributed Data Warehousing (DDW)". Being distributed objects/ components, we may also use the term "Object Oriented Data Warehousing" (OODW). The term "Distributed Knowledge Management System" may be used to denote all this.

9.2. DKMS Definition and Characteristics[1]

By definition, DKMS is one that manages the integration of distributed objects into a single functioning entity, producing, maintaining and enhancing a business knowledge base. A business knowledge base[2] comprises set of data, including rules, procedures and criteria, validated models, meta models and application software used for maintaining or processing them, pertaining to the enterprise. It may be produced either by using a DKMS or imported from other sources after creation of a DKMS. Thus, DKMS requires a knowledge base to begin operation. However, it enhances its own knowledge base, progressively, as a self-correcting system, continuously testing itself against real experience.

The scope of DKMS goes beyond a database or a data warehousing, as data is only a part of knowledge. It appeals to business domain as it can be used for better decision-making in business activities.

Individual islands of knowledge may be spread over the Internet. Just as a web-based data warehouse integrates data marts distributed over Internet, DKMS integrates knowledge bases, spread over the Internet. Thus, the problems of islands of knowledge will be overcome by DKMS.

Individual islands of data are expected to be integrated into one single enterprise database by a DBMS. Individual data marts are expected to be integrated into a single Data Warehouse. Individual knowledge repositories are to be merged into one – these goals are not so easily met. Hence, DKMS is aimed at achieving this integration.

9.3. How to Create a DKMS?

DKMS can be created *ab initio*, or starting from a pre-existing base of varied applications and relatively disparate (unintegrated) components. To create DKMS from the scratch will be quite expensive and more time consuming and more resource consuming than the process of creating a Data Warehouse. Therefore, it is more prudent to create DKMS by integrating existing components. Subsequently, we can add new components such as a Data Warehouse or a set of data marts as necessary from time to time. In the long term, an incremental approach to enhance a DKMS can be adopted to increase its size and complexity.

An incremental approach shall concentrate and focus on segmenting the DKMS process by process, sub-process by sub-process and use case by use case. Batch increment could then represent an implementation of a set of use cases found within a process, a sub-process or spanning across many sub-processes.

Similar to Software Development Life Cycle (SDLC), DKMS creation will comprise:

(a) Requirement identification and analysis,

(b) Identification of business objectives and goals of the Enterprise,

(c) Identification of process and sub process involved, and

(d) Identification of use cases.

9.4. Identifying Business Objectives and Goals of the Enterprise

The business objectives and the goals of the Enterprise become the fundamental basis on which the architecture of business processes, including processes and sub-processes can be defined. Processes and sub-processes are value streams whose purpose is to accomplish the declared business objectives and goals of the Enterprise. The strategic and actual goals may be expressed as an analytic hierarchy.[3] Analytic hierarchy orders a number of disjoint set of goals and objectives according to the absolute dominance of one set over the other. In Enterprise level planning, it is always better to specify first the tactical and strategic goals and objectives, then group these objectives into disjoint sets and then order these disjoint sets according to their dominance relations. By using the well known ratio scaling methods[4], particular states of objectives in the analytic hierarchy may be given numerical ratio scaled values. After such an analytic hierarchy is formed with values, business processes and use cases (formed separately), these may individually be evaluated in terms of their actual contribution and impact on the tactical objectives. This exercise at the Enterprise level may be very large and significant in its importance.

9.5. Major Sub-system Definition

The organisational sub-divisions are the major sub-systems of the Enteprise. Primary business processes flow through such sub-divisions of the organisation (e.g., Headquarters, Regional Office, State level offices, District level offices, etc., account for a National level organisation with country wide spread). All the end sub-systems may be involved in delivering a particular service, e.g., IT Services.

9.5.1. Business Process

A Business Process is a sequence of inter-related activities that transform given inputs into specified outputs.

Processes are value streams as they produce value to the organisation. They produce outcomes that are positively or negatively valued.

Different Enterprises have different processes. In an IT service, Enterprise delivery of different types of IT Services comprise different processes such as delivery of training to users, delivery of network services, delivery of software services, etc.

9.5.2. Sub-process as a Process

Any business process has at least four sub-processes: Planning, Acting, Monitoring and Evaluation.

Planning comprises of setting goals, objectives and priorities, making forecasts, performing cost/benefit experiments, reengineering a business process, documenting them, etc.

Acting comprises the performance or the actual execution of the business process.

Monitoring means tracking and describing the execution of the business process.

Evaluating comprises assessment of the performance of the business process as a value stream.

9.5.3. Actors

1. User: An external user of a business system is an individual or organisation outside the logical boundary of the area of Enterprise business being modelled, who uses a business process or a system e.g., a customer of a IT services organisation is outside the organisation but makes use of the services of the organisation.

2. Business System Actor: A Business System Actor is a particular coherent cluster of activities adopted by a user in relation to a business system – process. These structured sets of activities or roles played by users are what are termed as Business System Actors.

Actor concept is an abstraction from the basic notion of user and refers to an external delivery such as a source.

3. Information System Actors: A Business Process may be supported by a sub-process or sub-system called Information System.

Information System Actors are users who are external to the logical boundary of the Information System and who play coherent roles in the business system. Such business system actors may never use the information system directly but may always interface with others who, in turn, interface with information system. The original business system actors are not information system actors because they do not directly use the system. The individuals they may interface with may not be the business system actors because they may play roles in the business system that place them inside its logical boundaries, e.g., employees of the organisation.

The "business objects" who interface with the information system on behalf of the business system actors are actors relative to the information system, i.e., they are the users who play definable roles in connection with the information system and they are external to it, even if they are inside the business system.

9.5.4. Use Cases

A business system use case is defined by Jacobson as "a sequence of transactions in a system whose task is to yield a result of measurable value to an individual actor of the business system".

An information system use case, on the other hand, is defined by Jacobson as "a behaviourally related sequence of transactions performed by an actor in a dialogue with a system to provide some measurable value to the actor".

A behaviourally related set of information system use cases, in turn, constitutes an information systems application supporting a business process through its use cases (This application may or may not extend over the four sub-processes depending on its scope).

A use case is intended to accomplish some tactical objective of an actor or to aid in accomplishing a tactical objective. The use case concept focuses on the user's view point about what the system is supposed to give back in response to user's input, i.e., it is supposed to give back a response or output and that output will have value relative to a hierarchy of tactical and strategic objectives and goals.

The use case provides an external view of the system from the viewpoint of the users and their business processes. If a system is built on the foundation of use cases specified by the users, then these use cases lead us to objects and interactions and give rise to objects defined at higher levels be traceable down to the level of implemented code. Thus, it can be stated that the whole system architecture will be determined by the use cases and ultimately by the users who specified them. To recognise or modify the system, we can ask users to make the desired changes in use cases (add/delete/modify). Then, we can determine the schedule of development in iterative cycles by asking users about the priority among the various use cases defined.

Use Case Modelling is essential in constructing DKMS, because it leads to the identification of the actors performing the execution of the use cases and objects supporting it. Once the objects are identified, they, their relations, their interactions and dynamics can be modelled. Code can then be generated or hand written and then tested against the use cases, until an acceptable application results. Use cases are also essential in arriving at increments of the DKMS, in the incremental approach.

9.6. Requirement Analysis

Requirement Analysis comprises partitioning use cases into various objects supporting them. Modelling objects including their structural relations is required to be done.

9.7. Object Model for the Enterprise

Object model for the Enterprise is developed through four sub-models as indicated below:

(i) The Enterprise Business Object Sub-Model,

(ii) The Local Business Object Sub-Model,

(iii) The Interface Object Sub-Model, and

(iv) The Storage Object Sub-Model

We shall delve deeper into each of these.

The Enterprise Business Object Sub-Model (EBOM) shows the various object classes in the Enterprise System and their relations. An object is an identifiable unit of analysis of which properties may be predicated. The properties of an object are its attributes. We can also say an object is an entity in the enterprise with its attributes. All entities are to be identified as objects with attributes. Objects can be interrelated e.g., as an aggregation or as a class-subclass hierarchy with inheritance of attributes. Objects can have activity related to each other. These activities could be Processes in the Enterprise.

An input object will be processed by a process and an output object will be produced. A process can be a service or even represented as a web service. This model is given as Object Knowledge Model (OKM)[5]. Whatever be the model Enterprise, objects within attributes and interrelationship have to be defined. Activities or processes involving sub-objects also have to be defined. An object type is a description of a set of objects (instances) sharing the same attributes, operations and relationships. Object types have sub-types (classes are implementation of types in software). Objects are instances of types and are instances of classes in software.

The objects described as above, therefore, when generalised, are also examples of object types and when implemented become instances of classes.

A well known abstract typology of objects is that of interface, control and entity objects.[6] Interface objects are those that manage inputs to and outputs from an information system. Control objects coordinate objects interaction in one or more use cases. Entity objects manage information, resources and access to them within an information system.

More generally, object types encapsulate data and therefore have attributes. Objects are instances of object types whose attributes have values. Objects perform and also have operations performed on them. Objects also encapsulate methods that perform their operation which may be specified in code.

9.7.1. Components

A component is a large grained object. A component may be comprised of clusters of highly related small or smaller grained objects. Alternatively, a legacy procedure could be wrapped with a component providing an object interface and encapsulation to the legacy application.

Object Modelling begins with identifying and specifying Enterprise level business objects supporting business processes, sub-processes and use cases. Specification means identifying and describing object attributes, behaviour (operation) and methods. Objects specified will include the goals and objectives of the analytic hierarchy, as these are linked to other objects through the business processes and use cases and enterprise level business policies expressed as business rules.

When such rules have to be expressed explicitly, it can be done using OKM (Object Knowledge model) more elegantly than expressing in a rule base or an expert system or knowledge base system. OKM (5) can serve as a common model for both object model definitions and also knowledge representation. Prior to OKM, only the independent methodology had to be used to represent data objects and knowledge comprising rules, frames, etc.

OKM provides a common means to model and represent both knowledge and objects.

The Enterprise Business Object Sub-Model (EBOM) has to be defined showing relations among the enterprise business objects. It should include possible cause-effect relations (a type of an association) among objects, as these will be relevant later in identifying causal dimensions of the data warehouse and creating the necessary background of data mining activity (cause-effect is an important relationship between objects).

The Local Business Object Sub-Model (LBOM) shows the various objects in a business area system and their relationships. It comprises the same kinds of relations as in the enterprise wide model, but is specific to the business system under consideration for development or reengineering. Business Rules are an important aspect. An important sub-system of LBOM is the Information System Sub-Model.

Developing LBOM begins with identifying and specifying local business objects supporting the business processes, sub-processes and use cases. These are objects specific to the business area being analysed or the data mart. Specification means identifying and describing object attributes, behaviour (operation) and methods. Objects specified will include goals and objectives of the extended analytical hierarchy as these are linked to other objects through business processes and use cases and policies expressed as rules.

Next, we have to build LBOM showing relations among LBOs, including cause and effect relations.

The Interface Object Sub-Model (IOM) specifies the forms, controls, input fields, buttons and other objects in the GUI environment that users interact with when they begin work through and end use cases. It also specifies interface mechanisms such as mouse(s), keyboard(s), servers, printers, etc. The IOM is specified through diagrams, animated prototypes, GUIs and also as rapid prototypes with a real GUI developed in an IDE. Data Warehouse/data mart reporting and OLAP tools are also used to prototype IOM.

9.7.2. Storage Object Modelling

The Storage Object Modelling (SOM) specifies how storage is provided for data used by all objects inside the Information System. The model may be specified with ER relationships, data dictionaries, DDL Schemes, data locations and transaction relations. If an OODBMS is utilised for storage management, the storage object model is just a revised version of LBOM, optimised for performance.

If DBMS being used is relational i.e., RDBMS or extended RDBMS, then the model SOM can be as a Dimensional Data Model (DDM). Alternatively, we can use an OODBMS[7] or MDDBMS with a dimensionally oriented SOM specified to support rapid query performance. Object Oriented Software Engineering (OOSE)[8] approach with its associated object modelling provides a particularly systematic viewpoint for both conventional E-R and dimensional data modelling. Some relations developed in the object model provide a specific guide to the tables and relationships in a conventional ER model, other relations can provide a guide to tables and relationships in a dimensional data model. Identification of causal dimension in DDMs is particularly facilitated by object modelling, because tracing use cases to objects supporting them naturally leads to identifying the entity objects whose attributes may possibly determine the transactional sequences on tactical objectives.

9.7.3. System Design

System design invokes the process of adopting the requirements analysis to the specific physical environment of DKMS application. This begins with object interaction modelling and then continues with dynamic modelling of the life cycle of important objects, includes detailed design of architecture (client/server or central server) more detailed specification of previous models developed, including physical specification of database models and selecting tools for system development.

9.8. Object Interaction Modelling (OIM)

Object Interaction Modelling (OIM) specifies data flow, communication flow and transaction flow among the LBOM, EBOM, IOM and SOM objects or external actor supporting a use case. OIM is expressed when we specify use cases in detail through sequence diagrams correlating use case component tasks with message flows between the objects. The OIM cross references use cases and the objects supporting them. It is a key modelling constraint linking use cases and the four object sub models (described above).

Build an Object Interaction Model specifying data and other transactions and communication flow among the LBOM, EBOM, IOM and SOM objects or external actors supporting a use case. OIM may include object from LBOM to support use cases where data or causal measurement and predictive models are communicated from the business area data marts to the data warehouse.

9.9. Dynamic Modelling

Dynamic Model specifies the responses business and information system objects make to events. It models the "life cycle" of the objects. A set of State Transaction Diagrams (STDs) are used by the Dynamic Model. A State Diagram is a network of states and events, just an object diagram is a network of classes and relationships. One STD is developed for each object type where dynamic activity we think is important to represent. The arcs of a state diagram are activities and nodes are specific events.

While the object model describes the states of a system, such as a data warehousing information system at a point in time, the dynamic model describes changes in objects over time in response to events (messages transmitted from one object to another). Causal relationships identified in the Object Model may be implicated in the Dynamic Model by specifying Causal events and depicting the changes in state they produce. The causal relationship with the most significant effect attributes viewed from a business standpoint are the ones most important to explicate the dynamic model. We can pick these out by examining the analytic hierarchy and evaluating candidate relationships or hypothesis, according to whether they express goals and objectives in the hierarchy as effects.

The STDs should include the dynamic of process of extracting, transforming, transporting data to the data warehouse or data mart or application (as data mining).

9.9.1. Detailed Design of Object Types, Relationships and Interactions

We need to specify EBOM and/or LBOMs, OIMs and Dynamic Models in great detail. We also need to utilise other design techniques as Use Case Maps (a virtual notation aid to represent and reason about large grained behaviour patterns in system and to provide high level design tool to develop a better basis for specifying OIDs and collaboration groups to specify more details of use cases). We need to create more detailed Dynamic Models, review Use Case Maps and Sequence Diagrams as a foundation for extending Dynamic Models through more detailed STDs.

9.9.2. SOM Database Dictionaries and Schema

We need to create physical SOM database dictionaries and schema, specifying the physical dimensional data model or object model (if an OODBMS is used).

9.9.3. Detailed IOM Prototypes

We need to create detailed IOM Prototypes for user validation of the various IOMs defined in Enterprise level and/or business area analysis. As detailed IOM prototypes are implemented, the prototype begins to approach GUI implementation.

9.9.4. System Development

Using a variety of tools including Interactive Development Environment (IDE), code generators, coding system development can be completed along with system integration, data manipulation and processing, database turning, testing, installing and validating tasks such as Extracting, Transforming and Loading data (ETL).

Finally, the DKMS is implemented.

9.9.5. Standard Dialogues

A list of categories of standard dialogues could include:

- Analytic hierarchies of goals and objectives,
- Planning scenarios connecting action options to tactical objectives and indirectly to strategic objectives,
- Work flows assembling action sequences into strategic and tactical plans,
- Model applications to derive new predictions from data using existing models,
- Maintenance, basic information and complex segmentation responding to quick count and ad hoc queries,
- Impact analysis and/or forecasting of the properties and outcomes of previous activity,

- Assessing outcomes against tactical objectives,
- Assessing forecast outcomes against tactical objectives and forecast tactical objectives,
- Assessing benefits and costs of past and current activities and outcomes,
- Assessing forecast benefits and costs of future activities and outcomes,
- Batch data maintenance and updates,
- Batch cleaning and consolidation of server databases,
- Application partitioning and load balancing, and
- Security and access.

9.10. Conclusion

In this chapter, we have presented DKMS architecture, modelling and processes.

References

1. DKMS: The Next Wave in DSS, Joseph M Firestone, White Paper No. 6, Aug. 1997.
2. Intelligent Systems for Business (Belmont, CA, Wadsworth, 1993).
3. Analytical Hierarchies, Thomas L Saaty, http://www.expertchoice.com
4. The Analysis Hierarchy Process, Thomas L Saaty, RWS Publication, Pittsburgh, PA, 1990.
5. Prabhu CSR and Reddy Bhaskara: "Object Knowledge Model (OKM) for Semantic Description of Web Services in a Semantic e-Governance Grid", pp. 36-38, International Journal of Systemics, Cybernetics and Informatics, July, 2010. IFSN 0973-4864.
6. Jacobson, *et al.*, 1992, pp. 169-187.
7. Object Oriented Software Engineering (OOSE), Jacobson, et al, 1992.
8. Object Oriented Database System, Approaches and Architecture (3rd edition) by CSR Prabhu, published by PHI Learning, New Delhi.

10

Semantic Networks and Object Knowledge Model (OKM) for Semantic Web and Knowledge Management

Semantic Web or Web 3.0 is the new generation of the World Wide Web (WWW) based on knowledge representation mechanism with semantic network models or other models as OKM (Object Knowledge Model) (5).

Semantic network model enables representation of knowledge in terms of object – attribute – value triplet statements and Object Knowledge Model (OKM) enables representation of knowledge in terms of object–activity–attribute—value details.

10.1. Semantic Networks and OKM for Semantic Web Search

In the case of semantic networks by assuming that the terms used in object-attribute-value triplet statements are based on the formally specified meaning for the community of interest, i.e., ontologies, these triplets can be semantically processed by machine agents. Similarly Search engine based on OKM can be used for semantic web search. Most of the current semantic web applications are based upon using such atomic statements as pure facts, which we can reason about. So a machine agent can understand that a particular patient suffering with a disease X can be treated by the medicine Y. This information can be used by other agents for actions such as fixing an appointment with the Doctor, etc.

Moreover atomic statements could be conjuncted as joints with preconditions (such as "if the patient is female and is suffering from symptom 's' then the medicine 'm'can be given as the treatment"). On the implementation level this logic can be represented in "if-then-else" clauses or as rules. Then such rules or clauses can be processed by an appropriate rule engine or inference engine. The above process can be made use for knowledge represented using semantic network or even by using OKM.

From the end user point of view to have machine process-able knowledge statements as above means the possibility of performing knowledge search, processing knowledge and drawing inferences on the knowledge for the input given by the user, thus solving the problem as required by the user. Moreover conditional statements can be used for indexing the content of web resources in a more expressive way than simple conjunction of keywords (concepts or general metadata including relations). That will enable the formation of more sophisticated, content-aware queries and consequently it can improve precision and recall in the search for knowledge on the semantic web.

In processing such conditional statements it will be essentially required to have machine representation of all such "knowledge" so that "machine understandable" knowledge representation can be made for subsequent processing.

10.2. Knowledge Managementin Semantic Web

When we examine knowledge management scenario on the semantic web, such machine representability and machine processibility of knowledge is essential along with powerful mechanisms and engines or agents to manipulate and process such knowledge. Conditional and relational information or "knowledge" can be represented in the OKM or semantic networks or even by using RDFS format. RDF Rule (10.2) is the RDFS format for representing rules. Such representation enables the representation of knowledge in Horn Clauses as rules, extended by auncertainty factor and also model/context information. Since each rule contains a set of premises and a set of conclusions (both sets can be empty), the proposed RDFS format can be used for the description of conditional statements in the form of Pre-condition Actions ("if-then"). An application framework for managing knowledge resources on the semantic web for knowledge search and processing is also available (10.1). This framework is based on existing tools for semantic web (Ont O Mat, Ont O Mat – SOEP AND OntOMat-REVERSE, OntOMat-CRAWL, Omobroker) which are required to be extended, in order to operate with more expressible data format (conditional statements).

The knowledge management framework is as follows:

10.3. The Knowledge Management Framework[1]

The main process in a knowledge management system are (a) the possibility to find knowledge sources, which are relevant for the problem at hand and (b) the process of providing knowledge sources, which can be used in resolving the problem. From the point of view of the knowledge formalisation, these knowledge sources can be divided into two categories: (i) formal expert rules and (ii) (multi-media) documents. In order to enable more efficient searching for the knowledge that is contained in the second category, the content of the documents is indexed by using some ontology-based statements. These statements may have conditional form: Precondition-Action, which enables us to use the same logical mechanisms in the management of both categories of knowledge sources. Moreover, a search for relevant knowledge can result in some expert rules and/or some documents.

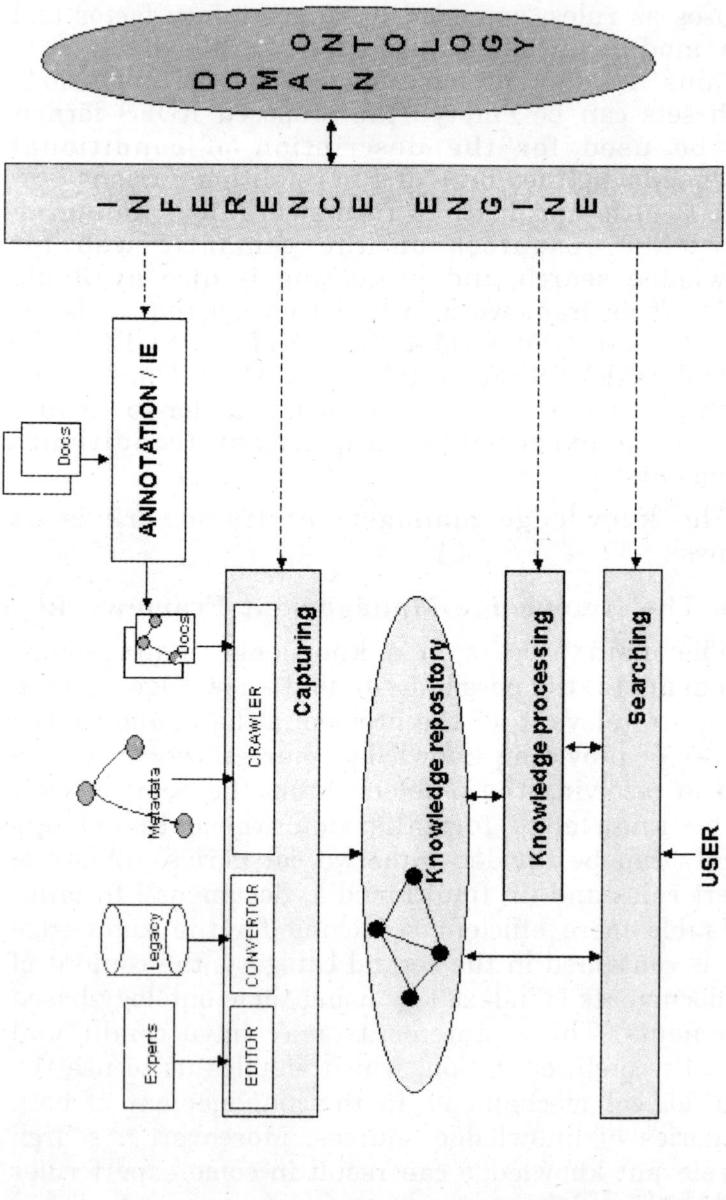

Fig. 10.1: Knowledge Management Framework on the Semantic Web.

The Fig. 10.1 sketches the Framework for Knowledge Management on the Semantic Web, which reflects the variety of knowledge transformations in this distributed environment: knowledge can be collected from various sources and in different formats, then stored in the common representation formalism, processed in order to compute interdependencies between knowledge items or to resolve conflicts, shared/searched and finally used for problem solving.

Therefore, this knowledge management approach encompasses the following processes (10.3):

1. Knowledge Capturing
2. Knowledge Representation
3. Knowledge Processing
4. Knowledge Sharing and
5. Using of Knowledge.

All processes are related somehow to domain ontology. Since ontology is a domain model, it contains a set of domain axioms which are used for deriving new information – that is the task of an inference engine. In the following section these processes are described:

1. Four types of knowledge sources can be identified, which could be treated in the knowledge capturing phase: expert knowledge, legacy (rule-based) systems, metadata repositories and documents. For each of them we can associate Semantic Web tools:

   (a) Expert knowledge in the form of rules can be captured using our Simple Ontology Editor Plug-In – OntOMat SOEP, an ontology editor that is extended with rule-editing capabilities. SOEP provides structure as well as vocabulary, i.e., lexical layer of the domain ontology, for the rule creation. Although these rules are related to domain ontology, they are not treated as axioms in that ontology. The ontological axioms should be always-true statements, which is not the case for expert rules. SOEP saves rules directly in the RDFRule format.

(b) Legacy rule-bases are very valuable sources of sharable knowledge, which can be consulted in solving some problems, either for free or for some price. The focus is not on collaborative problem solving via querying the federation of rule bases, but in creating high-specific expert bases, by importing relevant (for the given task) rule chains from those rule bases. The prerequisite is to have a mechanism to convert legacy rule-bases into rule-interlingua. The potential candidate for the common-accepted rule mark-up is RuleML (10.4). OntOMat-REVERSE, the tool which translates the content of a relational database into an ontology represented in the RDF can be used for the support of this translation into RDFRule.

(c) Metadata spread on the web should be the primary knowledge source for sharing knowledge in the future. In order to make that sharing more efficient some mechanisms for knowledge packaging and knowledge trading/ pricing are needed (10.5). OntOMat-CRAWL, ontology-focused and metadata-aware crawler already has the capabilities to collect web documents (metadata) that fit the given "knowledge" model, so that the adaptation to rule-crawling is straightforward.

(d) The previous three types are related to formally stated knowledge, which can be processed by machine agents. Knowledge in the documents is informally represented, but the content of a document can be formally stated by ontology based indexes. The underlying process is called semantic annotation and it is supported by OntOMat annotation framework (10.6). By using some information extraction (IE) techniques it is possible to make annotation semi-automatically. For example, it is possible to extend OntOMat with techniques for the extraction of the tabular content in order to convert tabular information into a set of rules automatically.

2. Knowledge repository is a relational database organised in a way that enables efficient storing and access to RDF metadata. This repository can be seen as a RDF repository.
3. Knowledge processing component enables efficient manipulation with the stored knowledge, especially graph-based processing for the knowledge represented in the form of rules, e.g. deriving dependency graph or consistency checking
4. Knowledge sharing is realised by searching for rules that satisfy the query conditions. In the RDF repository rules are represented as RDF statements and while in RDF any statement is considered to be an assertion, we can view an RDF repository as a set of ground assertions in the form (subject, predicate, and object). Rules are also related to domain ontology, which contains domain axioms used for deriving new assertions. Therefore the searching is realised as an inference process. Ontobroker, a main memory, deductive, object oriented database system can be used, which inferences using RDF inputs also. To note that this system treats facts and queries

as rules without the rule body and the rule head, respectively. This facility enables using the SOEP editor as a query interface.

5. Using the knowledge is related to semantic web-enabled knowledge portals scenarios[3] The main advantage of this approach is using a conditional statement for the semantic annotation of knowledge sources. In that way we put statements used in the annotation into the context of each other, which consequently leads to efficient searching for knowledge. Moreover, annotating knowledge resources using Precondition-Action statements enables semantic hyperlinking of each two resources, which satisfies the condition that the Precondition part of one annotation; subsumes the Action part of the annotation of another resource. In that way querying for a problem can result in a composition of documents, which cover problem solving. This is a very important process in knowledge management or e-learning search.

10.4. Conclusion

In this chapter an application framework for realising a Knowledge Management system on the Semantic Web is presented. The proposed framework is mainly based on existing Semantic Web tools. The approach introduces two new aspects, which could enhance applicability of the Semantic Web tools in real-world applications: (i) rules as the first class citizens on the Semantic Web and (ii) semantic annotation by using conditional statements. The benefits of the proposed approach are manifold: an integration platform for various rules sources and rules format, more precise search for knowledge sources by using conditional statements, machine-processable description of the content of the tabular- and graphic-based resources, a possibility to compose various knowledge sources in solving some rare difficult tasks.

References

1. N. Stojanovic, Siegfried Hand Schuh. A framework for knowledge management on semantic web. AIFB Institute, University of Karlsruhe, D-76131, Karlsruhe, Germany.
2. N. Stojanovic, Siegfried. Searching knowledge in the Semantic Web. FLAIRS 2002, Special track on Semantic Web.
3. S. Staab, H.P. Schnurr, R. Studer, Y. Sure: Knowledge Processes and Ontologies. IEEE Intelligent Systems. 16(1)
4. N. Stojanovic, A. Maedche, S. Staab, R. Studer, Y. Sure. SEAL — A Framework for Developing Semantic Portals. ACM K-CAP, 2001. October, Vancouver.
5. CSR Prabhu, T Bhaskar Reddy. OKM (Object Knowledge Model) for Knowledge Representation and semantic search on web pages abstracts comprising simple sentences.

Case Studies

Case Study No. 1
Infosys Technologies Limited

Infosys was founded in 1981. It is an Indian software services company with headquarters in Bangalore. Growing consistently since its inception by nearly 70 per cent it became the first Indian company to be listed on the NASDAQ in 1999.

Organisation's Business Goals

- To be the pioneer in the field of software.
- Deliver high quality services.
- Responsive to customer needs.
- Thrive in a highly competitive environment.

Major Products and Services of the Company

- Finance
- Planning
- Marketing
- Quality
- Human resources
- Education and research
- Information systems

Gap between Existing Knowledge and Required Market Demand

- Lack of educated and trained employees

- Lack of motivation to use KM systems.
- KM systems and processes not used frequently.

KM Tools and Strategies Used to Overcome Challenges

- **The KM portal:** A central repository for content
- The people knowledge map: A directory service for locating experts.
- **The knowledge exchange:** A set of online discussion forums.
- **K-Mail:** An auto response generator and work - flow engine for answering questions.
- **K-agent:** An intelligent assistant for authoring documents.

Prompts the writer with content from the KM repositories to what is being written

- **K-classify:** A tool for automatically classifying a submitted knowledge asset according to the corporate taxonomy.
- **K-desktop:** An environment for preparing a document to be submitted at the repository as a knowledge asset.
- **K-enterprise:** A business intelligence application for analysing and viewing KM measurements.
- K-Mark: An enterprise repository through which people can share their intranet or internet bookmarks, classify them and search and browse through others published bookmark collections.
- **K-speak:** An interactive voice response interface for querying the knowledge portal over the telephone.
- **K-subscribe:** An application for creating customised subscriptions to the knowledge portal to receive automatic notifications about new content relevant to the interest.

- **K-summarize:** A tool for automatically generating the summary of a document or a web page.

Different Processes Operating

Publication Process:

- Each K-asset which meets certain standards have to undergo publication.
- Minimum readability standards.
- Intellectual property rights requirements.

Review Process

- Assets published on the KM portal undergo review process to ascribe proper quality rating to the assets.
- Done by the experts.
- Proper communication between authors and reviewers.
- Public comments are provided to the assets.

Rating Process:

- Any employee may rate any asset on the KM portal.
- Aggregate ratings are collectively updated.
- Any asset falling below the rating is removed from the repository.
- Review process meant for experts but rating process is for any users.
- Review process is run only once at the time when the asset is published but rating process is run throughout the published life of the asset.

Subscription Process and Personalisation Process:

- User can create one or more subscriptions to personalise the content they see.

- Based on the ratings the top ranking assets can be selected for subscriptions.
- Subscription process requires getting updates about new contents added for the relevant areas.

Reward Process

- Incentives and awards are presented to the selected employees with highest composite scores.

Forms of Knowledge

- Explicit knowledge.
- Tacit knowledge.
- Group knowledge.
- Individual knowledge.
- Internal knowledge.
- External knowledge.

Methods to Extract Knowledge

- Transfer of knowledge: Intranet portal called K-shop enables to access the contents from their desktops.
- Reuse of knowledge: To reduce time pressure.
- Internal and external sensing: Two internal consulting groups-
    - Domain Competency Group-covers industry dynamics, trends, and key-players.
    - Software engineering and technology labs.-develop technology architecture and frameworks.
- Proximity centers at different geographical locations: So that Infosys can access local knowledge while operating globally.
- Creating or capturing knowledge: Corporate taxonomy is a set of hierarchies of knowledge areas known as K-nodes.
- Organising, storing and sharing knowledge.

Case Study No. 2

Airtel Broadband

Bharti Airtel limited, a part of Bharti enterprises, is one of India's leading private sector providers of telecommunication services with an aggregate of 30.27 million customers.

Organisation's Business Goals

- Maximising revenues and margins.
- Enhancing customer satisfaction.
- Build competitive advantage through human resource development.
- Leverage on the strengths of strategic and financial partners like Singtel, Vodafone, New York life insurance.

Major Products and Services of the Company

- Mobile telephone services
- Broadband and telecommunication services
- Enterprise services.

Gap between Existing Knowledge and Market Demand

- Lack of skilled manpower.
- Local and regional variables.
- Ever-changing environment.

Strategies and Tools Used to Overcome Challenges

- KM is the primary tool. Insights@Airtel was launched to solve the issues.
- Key performance indicators.
- Process audits.
- Six sigma projects.
- Documentation and publication of best practices.
- Knowledge sharing sessions.

- Exploit available internal knowledge.

Forms of Existing Knowledge

- Explicit knowledge.
- Tacit knowledge.
- Individual knowledge.
- Group knowledge.

Methods to Extract Knowledge

- **Internal and External Sensing:** People are encouraged to add explicit content to the appropriate repositories. People can share their knowledge and ideas.
- **Creating or capturing knowledge**:
  1. Each repository has K-champs and subject matter experts to encourage knowledge sharing and they are available to answer questions related to their domains.
  2. This ensures that tacit knowledge of the experts can be tapped to solve business problems.
  3. For explicit knowledge a non financial repository was created.

     Monthly performance of all business units is tracked and ranked based on the chosen criteria.
  4. Top performing units will share the good practices while low performing units are expected to replicate the best practices.
- **Organising, Storing, and Sharing Knowledge**:
  1. There is no single predefined KM process. Each organisation must proceed along its own learning curve and discover what is best suited.

2. The KM process had the following points:

- Simple, fast, user-friendly processes for sharing knowledge.
- Standard formats designed to maximum replication value.
- Knowledge-sharing sessions.
- Virtual collaborations, team rooms, threaded discussions.

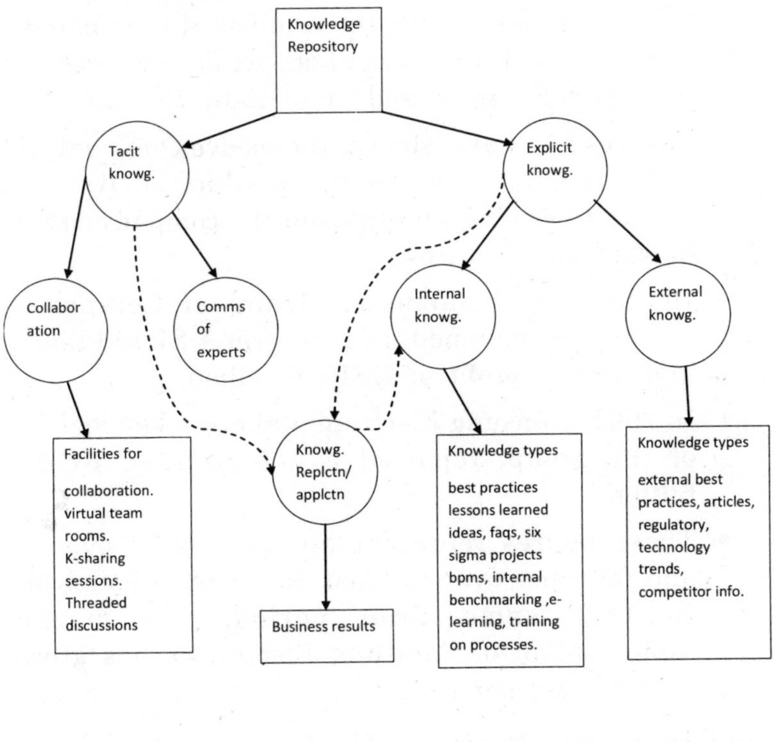

Case Study No. 3

SAMSUNG ADVANCED INSTITUTE OF TECHNOLOGY (SAIT)

- The Samsung Group of Companies consists of over 60 different affiliate companies in four broadly defined industrial sectors: Electronics, Finance, Machinery and Chemicals and Trade and Services
- Samsung has secured its leadership position in a number of products, including memory chips and TFT-LCD. Since 1999, the number of local patents has increased over sevenfold, while international patents have increased more than 15 times.
- The results have shown themselves not only in the laboratory and on the product shelves but also in their sales, profits and the company's stock market share prices.
- In 2003, the Samsung Group of Companies reported a combined sales of over USD100 billion and a total profit of USD5.6 billion.
- In 2004, Samsung Electronics alone, a key member of the group, reported a net profit of USD10 billion.
- These figures represent an increase of over 10 and 50 times over the last 10 years, respectively. In that same time period, the market capitalisation of Samsung Electronics has grown by over 700 per cent.

Organisation's Business Goals

Samsung Advanced Institute of Technology (SAIT), established as the group's central Research and Development facility since 1987, has made critical contributions to ensure the Samsung Group's position as the leading edge of technology. This case study presents the story of SAIT and its knowledge management (KM) activities.

Main Goals

1. Fusion and synergy to facilitate Samsung's leadership in the age of convergence.
2. Dominant design development efforts to develop leading standards in the rapidly changing technological environment.
3. Research and Development maximisation from both effectiveness and efficiency perspectives.

Major Products and Services of the Company

- Industrial sectors:
- Electronics
- Finance
- Machinery
- Chemicals and
- Trade and Services.

Samsung has Secured its Leadership Position in a Number of Products:

- Memory chips
- TFT-LCD.

Gap between Existing Knowledge and the Required Market Demand

- Lack of educated and trained employees
- Lack of motivation to use KM systems.
- KM systems and processes not used frequently.

KM Tools and Strategies Used to Overcome Challenges

Process-based KM

- One important characteristic of KM at SAIT is its process-based approach.
- This was a natural extension from SSP (SAIT Standard Process) established at SAIT before the KM efforts were introduced in 1999.

- SSP is now fully integrated into all — work, KM, and the Six Sigma-based processes at SAIT and serves as a standard process from concept generation to commercialisation.

Communities of Practice

- SAIT has looked into communities of practice (CoPs) to address these challenges.
- CoPs typically consist of employees from all over the organisation, regardless of their formal positions and immediate responsibilities.
- CoPs are now commonly accepted to be uniquely valuable in generating, sharing, and validating key knowledge.

Patent Expo

- A Patent Expo is open to all SAIT researchers; researchers from any research group of any technological background may choose to display research ideas and/or challenges in the Expo.

CRC and External Collaboration

- Considering the longer-term perspective, one of the major issues in SAIT's KM journey has always been that of collaboration with an external expert community.
- In other words, collaboration with the external expert community is a key factor for SAIT in attaining its strategic objectives.

The Cyber Research Centre

- The Cyber Research Center (CRC) is an essential element of KM at SAIT and has proved to be an especially effective means of collaboration with the expert community.
- CRC is the basic tool in which any and all research activities are to be recorded.

Cultural/ Behavioural Initiatives

- Conventional wisdom would suggest that a successful KM system requires a careful marriage between a set of KM systems and/or an infrastructure and a reinforcement mechanism.

Knowledge Intensive (KI) Staff Meetings

- Considering the nature of the organisation and its members, most of whom are highly educated and talented scientists and researchers, SAIT KM leaders agreed that even slightly coercive methods would be counterproductive.

Praise Ground

- KI meetings are supplemented by other means of internal communications. Praise Ground is a less formal means than KI meetings.
- It is designed to foster cross-functional and cross organisational boundary communications.

Different Processes Operating

- SAIT standard process: SSP
- Concept start
- Feasibility study
- Technology and process development
- Technology transfer
- Value for customer
- **Core Knowledge**
- *Knowledge identification:* Forecasting critical leading-edge technologies for the next five to ten years into the future.
- *Knowledge creation:* Conducting research to actualise the technologies of the future.
- *Knowledge delivery:* Tra©149

nsferring developed technologies to relevant Samsung affiliates for commercialisation.

Forms of Knowledge:

- Explicit knowledge.
- Tacit knowledge.
- Group knowledge.
- Individual knowledge

Methods to Extract Knowledge

Process Alignment

- The most important characteristic of SAIT KM is that it is fully integrated into work or, in SAIT's case, its research processes.
- The entire research process is divided into distinctive knowledge-generating phases.
- At each phase, generated knowledge is reported and stored in predefined formats for easy accumulation, sharing, and reutilisation: Core knowledge.

Cultural/ Behavioural Initiatives

- Knowledge is an inherently human factor.
- Even the most advanced system and rules cannot be employed successfully if they are not fully supported and accepted by the people in the organisation.

Monitoring KM Effectiveness

- It is always important to measure KM effectiveness.
- Through careful monitoring of KM activities and their impact on organisational performance, potential areas of weakness may be identified for proper corrective actions.

Case Study No. 4

BANK INDONESIA

The institutional history of Bank Indonesia began with the promulgation of Act No. 11/1953, the Outline Law on Bank Indonesia, which came into force on 1 July, 1953. In discharging its duties as the Central Bank of the Republic of Indonesia, the bank was managed by a monetary board, a board of directors, and an advisory board.

At the beginning of the new order era, the operational basis of Bank Indonesia was modified through Act No. 13/1968 by the central bank of the Republic of Indonesia. Since then, the Bank Indonesia has continued its function as the country's central bank and at the same time has assisted the government in its national development efforts by implementing the policies that it has adopted with the help of the monetary board. The board thus no longer manages the Bank Indonesia.

A new chapter in the history of Bank Indonesia as an independent central bank began when a new law, Act No. 23/1999 concerning Bank Indonesia, took effect on 17 May, 1999. This law provides Bank Indonesia with the status and position of a state institution that is independent and free from the interference of the government or other parties. As an independent state institution, Bank Indonesia enjoys full autonomy in formulating and exercising its every duty and authority as provided for under the law.

Organisation's Business Goals

- Maintain monetary stability.
- Maintain the financial sustainability of Bank Indonesia.
- Strengthen the effectiveness of monetary management.

- Create a sound and effective banking system and ensure the stability of the financial system.
- Maintain the security and effectiveness of the payment system.
- Increase the effectiveness of the implementation of good governance.
- Strengthen the organisation and build a corps of highly competent human resources with the support of a knowledge-based work culture.
- Integrate Bank Indonesia's transformation in line with its destiny statement of 2008.

Major Products and Services of the Company

- Monetary sector.
- Banking sector.
- Payment system sector.
- Internal management sector.

Gap between Existing Knowledge and the Required Market Demand

- Lack of motivation.
- Lack of educated and trained employees.
- Geographical variations.
- Adjustments must be made to local culture in order to make the entire workforce interested in and willing to use and participate in it.

KM Tools and Strategies Used to Overcome Challenges

- Formalised the KM initiative in the form of a project charter which shall be accounted for to the governor/senior deputy governor of the bank.
- Use of the participatory approach by involving employees in the process of change, assigning them a role and responsibility in the process; for example, the role of those in a leadership position

as a role model, the role as a partner for change.

- Establish the goals to be achieved in a detailed and specific way that include duties and responsibilities and behavioural changes expected for each role.
- Maintain persuasive, two-way communication channels aimed at providing understanding and receiving inputs and views from those affected by the change with regard to the KM concept.
- Conduct training and development programmes to fill in the gaps in required knowledge and skills with regard to the desired changes.
- Integrate the learning and sharing activities into the business process to make them a part of the working process that employees are able to relate to in their daily life.
- Formalise the desired changes into the regulations and policies of Bank Indonesia so that these can become institutionalised and be implementable.
- Knowledge LYNX is a repository of knowledge developed by the Bank as a result of key performance indicators for knowledge-sharing.

Different Processes Operating

- Time management.
- Creative thinking.
- Emotional management.
- Negotiation skills.
- Working as a team.
- Communication skills.
- Central banking studies.
- Inflation.
- Logistics management of Bank Indonesia.

Forms of Knowledge:

- Explicit knowledge.
- Tacit knowledge.
- Group knowledge.
- Individual knowledge.
- Internal knowledge.
- External knowledge.

Methods to Extract Knowledge:

Implementing Knowledge Share

Knowledge Share has currently been implemented in DKM and DPD; the process of work and working documents have been integrated into an enterprise content management system called Knowledge Share.

The benefits of implementing Knowledge Share are:

- Easy to use.
- Information available when needed.
- Enhanced customer relations.
- Reduction in costs.
- Reduction of redundant work.

Scope of Knowledge Share at DPD:

- e-Document.
- e-Process.
- Decision-making process.
- Reserve transaction.
- Intervention.
- Submission of reports for board of governors' meetings.

Scope of Knowledge Share at DKM:

- e-Document.
- e-Process.
- Submission of reports for board of governors' meetings.
- Research process.

Case Study No. 5

CHINA AMERICAN PETROCHEMICAL COMPANY

The China American Petrochemical Company, Ltd, CAPCO was founded in 1976 as a joint venture by two companies, the Purified Terephthalic Acid (PTA) process technology developers, BP and the CPC Corporation, Republic of China. After having been in the business for 30 years, CAPCO's capitalisation now stands at TWD7.072 billion.

Organisation's Business Goals

- To maintain quality.
- To maintain integrity.
- To train and develop people to reach their full potential for mutual benefit, and recognise every individuals' contribution to the team effort, measured by productivity, performance, and teamwork.

Major Products and Services of the Company

- Textile products-Use–Polyester fabrics, non-woven cloths, etc.
- Civil products-Use–PET bottles, videotapes, audiotapes, electrical wires,

Medical X-ray Films, Films, Resins, etc.

- Industrial products-Use—Polishers, Binders, Paints, Tire linings, Conveyor belts, safety belts.

Gap between Existing Knowledge and Required Market Demand

- In the KM system, PTA knowledge hall, search engine is not satisfactory.
- KM practice has been an extra workload for the employees.

- In the KM system, Management of change, the implementation time has been brief and there are no significant results yet.

KM Tools and Strategies Used to Overcome Challenges

- **Enterprise Resource Planning (ERP) of SAP**
  1. It is the enterprise resource planning system.
  2. There are some tools for KM applications; however it is not designed for KM.
- **PTA knowledge hall**
  1. Customised KM system by a software vendor.
  2. Search engine is not satisfactory.
  3. Supports five categories in manufacturing-operations, maintenance, quality, technical and control.
- **Management of change**
  1. Change management system, containing functions of planning, processing, and document archiving.
  2. The implementation time has been brief.
  3. Has three main functions:

  1. Risk evaluation: When a change project is initiated, the project manager or engineer evaluates and discusses the associated risk through the MOC system. The discussion process and all the related information are recorded.

  2. Change project design: The change project is planned and designed.

  3. Safety confirmation: Safety examinations and employee training must be confirmed before the project is carried out.

- **Share knowledge portal**
  1. Meeting arrangement system that provides functions such as schedule arrangement details, document storage, and full text searching.
  2. The ease and convenience in its use made employees to use it naturally.
- **Education training system**
  1. Education, training and certification system.
  2. Continuously increasing knowledge contents since established in 2000.
  3. The system is more convenient with abundant learning materials for employees.
  4. The Multimedia Cyber college was implemented in 2000 where there are more than 100 subjects all developed by with the company by CAPCO employees.
- **Centralised Database:** CAPCO had different databases used by various departments for their on-the-job functions. ERP requires that the databases be centralised. In addition, scattered paper documents had to be digitalised and stored. The search engine had to be improved. The webpage interface has to have a user-friendly design so that even employees with no programming skills could access the information. These actions paved the way KM practice.
- **Knowledge Identification**

1. In 2000, CAPCO assigned a knowledge management promotion committee to identify core knowledge and build a knowledge community.
2. While the system was somewhat lacking in terms of the KM function, KM promotional activities were successful in educating the employees to recognise the importance of KM.

- **Promotional Activities**
- Promotional activities are catalysts that accelerate employee reactions to the KM practice.
- There are two main promotion programmes at CAPCO.

1. **Business Unit Performance Review Meeting (BUPRM).**
   - Engineers and managers in various business units gather to share their experiences and exchange expertise.
2. **Certification Programme**
   - This programme is intended to measure the awareness of employees,
   - Especially operators in the field, of all the regulations pertaining to their work.
   - Employees continue working on further certification, advances in their skills and knowledge will enhance company productivity.

Forms of Knowledge

- Explicit knowledge.
- Tacit knowledge.

Methods to Extract Knowledge

Knowledge Communities

- CAPCO encouraged its employees to form teams for specific learning purposes but primarily for knowledge exchange and innovation.
- Through frequent interactions among team members by way of meetings, discussions, training, or sharing, tacit knowledge can be converted into explicit knowledge and thus lead to the formation of a KM culture.

- There are various teams in CAPCO: the reliability improvement team, the process technology network team, the safety team, etc.
- Employees are also encouraged to participate in knowledge communities with inter-department members.

Business Unit Performance Review Meeting (BUPRM)

- Engineers and managers in various business units gather to share their experiences and exchange expertise.

The Multimedia Cyber College

- Managers and experienced engineers were asked to share their expertise.
- The contributions were then edited into teaching materials in the form of articles, tables, figures, and computer animations that have been adopted to explain difficult and complex subjects.

Case Study No. 6

GOLDSUN COMPANY

- Founded in 1994, Goldsun has developed its capabilities in the field of marketing and communication design to specialise in multi-advertising services development.
- Being a member of the International Advertising Association (IAA) has helped Goldsun increase its knowledge about the advertising world and of its international standards.
- First Vietnamese advertising agency to be certified by ISO9001.
- One of only a few Vietnamese ad agencies to run TN market research software.
- PR and advertising synergy.
- Strong offices in key markets: Ha Noi and Ho Chi Minh City.
- Good relationship with media owners and favorable discount rates for clients.
- Industrious, young, creative, continuously trained team.

Organisation's Business Goals

- To become a leading company of its kind.
- To provide customers with error free advertising.
- To give top priority to the factors related to personnel and technology.

Major Products and Services of the Company

- Strategy and Branding.
- Creative graphic design.
- Outdoor advertising.
- TVC compose.
- Public relations.

- Brand consultancy service.
- Event promotion/sport marketing.
- Media plan-media buying.
- Sponsor marketing.
- Print.

Gap between Existing Knowledge and Required Market Demand

- There is insufficient content to encourage people to access the system. Goldsun's work encompasses a vast range of activities, so that a great deal of knowledge is created, but choosing the "right" knowledge for inclusion in the system is sometimes difficult.
- Absence of habits of sharing and learning. People are more familiar with traditional training, that is, acquiring knowledge and keeping it only for their own use without sharing it.

KM Tools and Strategies Used to Overcome Challenges

- *An organisational strategy:* Equitising and establishing a new company.
- *An expanded market strategy:* Transforming competitors into colleagues, developing strategic linkages.
- *Service diversity strategy:* Using flexibility to control diversity.
- *Personnel strategy:* People are the most valuable resource of the company. Goldsun has implemented a strategy to regard the company's employees as stakeholders, to employ outstanding individuals and treat them well, and to empower its employees.
- *Technology strategy:* Invest in advanced technology.

- Establishing a rule that employees must use the C2K for updating customer information and transactions via the controlling system of QMR before service contracts will be signed by the CEO.
- Granting rewards based on calculating points related to one's contribution to and sharing of knowledge within the system.
- *The KM implementation process:* The KM project was developed so that it would be consistent with corporate business goals. The KM team thus identified KM drivers and a KM vision that were in line with Goldsun business goals, and the KM objectives were then developed to achieve those goals.
- Different stages of implementation of KM project are:
  1. Planning.
  2. Knowledge mapping.
  3. Requirement analysis.
  4. System design and implementation.
  5. Content management.
  6. Measuring.
  7. Expansion.

Forms of Knowledge

1. Knowledge base on customers (KOC).
2. Knowledge base on services (KOS).
3. Knowledge base on lessons learned on sales/ marketing and consultancy (KOL).

Methods to Extract Knowledge

The KM team drew a knowledge map for sales/ marketing and consultancy knowledge. Goldsun places a great deal of emphasis on training. The KM team conducted interviews with various users. The primary question asked was how people acquire, store, share, and use knowledge to improve productivity. A great deal of knowledge will be put into systems; QMS, tables, figures, customer information and data in each service area, improvement, information related to the advertising field, regulations, supplier data, and other fields of knowledge considered to be the core competency.

Case Study No. 7

JTC CORPORATION

COMPANY PROFILE

- JTC Corporation (JTC) is Singapore's leading master planner and provider of industrial space solutions. It was established in 1968 and tasked to develop and manage industrial facilities in Singapore.
- Over the past 39 years, JTC has helped to power the growth of Singapore's economy by developing 7,000 hectares of industrial land and four million square meters of ready-built factories for more than 7,000 local and multi-national companies.
- JTC owns specialised parks, such as the Jurong Island, Wafer Fab (fabrication) parks, iomedical parks, and an airport logistics park.
- JTC has a staff of about 800 employees and places great emphasis on customer satisfaction and holistic talent management, as indicated by its involvement in the so-called FIREfly1 alliance. JTC has one of Singapore's most dynamic statutory boards, led by Chief Executive Officer Ow Foong Pheng.
- JTC first started as a builder of industrial land and facilities but then placed a stronger emphasis on the creation of entire industry clusters, in line with Singapore's cluster development approach.
- JTC closely collaborates with other Singaporean government agencies to develop attractive urban designs for different industry clusters that enhance the business environment of its customers.

Organisation's Business Goals

- Like many other statutory or government-linked

companies in Singapore, JTC's objective is to achieve organisational excellence.

- JTC places emphasis on innovation and encourages employees to proactively embrace new ideas and change.
- One strategic business goal is to maintain JTC's position as leader in the real estate industry, i.e., to increase productivity and to exceed customer needs.

Major Products and Services of the Company

- JTC offers a wide range of industrial and business facilities tailored to suit all types of manufacturing and related operations.
- Business facilities range from land preparations to ready-built factories that are fully serviced with basic infrastructure, quality finishes, innovative designs, functional layouts, and easy accessibility.
- Some of the new-generation products include stack-up factories, technopreneur centers, and incubators for start-up technology companies business parks, and science hubs.
- JTC owns specialised parks, such as Jurong Island, Wafer Fab (fabrication) parks, biomedical parks, and an airport logistics park.

Gap between Existing Knowledge and Required Market Demand

- Lack of motivation.
- Lack of educated and trained employees.
- Geographical variations
- Adjustments must be made to local culture in order to make the entire workforce interested in and willing to use and participate in it.
- Lack of natural resources

KM tools and Strategies Used to Overcome Challenges

Knowledge Strategy: Technology

- JTC emphasises web technology to support capturing, sharing, and creating knowledge.
- JTC has launched several employee portals:
- Platinum (JTC's intranet)
- Krypton (net for customers),
- Titanium (for partners and suppliers),
- The corporate website for the general public, and
- Virtual online communities for various industry clusters within JTC's clientele.

Knowledge Strategy: People

While technology must be in place to facilitate and support a knowledge-sharing environment—

For instance when face-to-face communication on a daily basis is not possible—it is human input, in combination with interests and perceived benefits, that drives any knowledge initiative.

JTC has attempted to kick-start and nurture the development of a knowledge-sharing culture is to encourage members to participate in different types of Communities of Practice (CoPs), in which every member is connected by JTC's extensive IT infrastructure.

Some examples of Communities of Practice that focus on issues are a Five-year Roadmap.

- Benchmarking,
- Crisis Management
- Project Portfolio Management
- Enterprise Workflow Engine,
- Facility Management.

Human Resource Management Practices

- The effectiveness of KM initiatives can be greatly improved through relevant, needs-based, up-to-date HRM practices.
- Through meaningful reward systems, employees can be motivated to engage in knowledge-sharing activities on a regular basis.
- At JTC, the Knowledge Activist award promotes and rewards employees' knowledge-sharing behaviour.
- The objective of the award is to promote a knowledge-sharing culture and practices in JTC and to recognise staff members who have made outstanding contributions to knowledge-sharing initiatives.

Dynamic Workspace

- In the case of JTC is its so-called Dynamic Workspace 3 solution that builds upon JTC's corporate culture.
- Learning before Doing: With the Dynamic Workspace, research into previous similar projects can be made before a new project starts.

Strategic Knowledge Leadership

KM in JTC is effectively driven and nurtured by top management via the CRKM department, which is linked to the corporate planning group.

Different Processes Operating

Implementation of change management and outreach activities to enhance staff awareness and commitment.

- Initial focus on groups that had implemented or were implementing customised workspaces (with Share point as the platform).

- Facilitation work aimed at kick-starting initiatives to start new workspaces, to enhance the participation of users, and to recruit new ones.
- Sharing of expertise and experiences among workspaces.

Exploring the Feasibility of "incentivising" Knowledge-sharing

- A corporate-wide taxonomy and metadatabase2 aimed at developing a structure that better organises JTC's knowledge assets and contents.
- A common platform, in the form of a "common contribution template," to simplify and standardise knowledge capturing and sharing processes.
- A powerful enterprise search engine which allows efficient and effective access to JTC's knowledge assets.

Forms of Knowledge

- Explicit knowledge.
- Tacit knowledge.
- Group knowledge.
- Individual knowledge: KM experts

Methods to Extract Knowledge

- Dynamic Workspace solutions typically deliver built-in expert knowledge about work-related correlation data and information in the form of context-sensitive on-screen links, enabling users to navigate with the click of the mouse to specific entries in relevant workspaces.
- An e-application template was created for employees to submit their budget and to get it approved online.
- To further ensure user-friendliness, previously approved and non-approved budgets were posted on the site for reuse and guidance.
- e-Document

Case Study No. 8

UNILEVER INDONESIA

- PT Unilever Indonesia, TBK (UI) was founded on 5 December, 1933 under the name Lever's Zeepfabrieken N.V.
- UI is one of some 400 publicly-listed companies in Indonesia.
- By 2003, the company had a sales of USD984 million, around 84 per cent of which were home and personal care items
- Around 16 per cent of sales were accounted for by food items.
- UI is ranked as the thirteenth-largest company in sales volume in Indonesia and the fourth-largest company in the Fast-Moving-Consumer-Goods (FMCG) sector.

Organisation's Business Goals

- To be the first and the best in its class in meeting the needs and aspirations of consumers.
- To be the closest in the market to the customers and suppliers.
- To remove non-value-added activities from all processes.
- To provide job satisfaction for all.
- To aim for lofty targets for profitable growth and secure above-average rewards for its employees and shareholders.
- To earn respect for its integrity and concern for the community and the environment.

Major Products and Services of the Company

- Home and personal care items such as soap powder, household cleaning products, hand soaps, and shampoos.

- Food items such as tea, margarine, and ice cream.
- Fast-Moving-Consumer-Goods (FMCG) sector.

Gap between Existing Knowledge and Required Market Demand

- Unwillingness to participate in learning programmes.
- Unwillingness to take the initiative for knowledge sharing.
- Less practical approach to Knowledge Management.

KM Tools and Strategies Used to Overcome Challenges

UI has Different Kinds of Communities of Practice (CoPs):

- K-Club shows—business sharing in the form of a talk show.
- Group of learning and development GLAD—a sharing forum among the youth.
- Book Club sharing—some people read a book and share it with others; the outcome of the discussion is captured and documented in the K-Club site.
- Sharing of learning and discussions (SOLAR)—UI invites prominent leaders from outside the company to share their invaluable knowledge.
- A video cafe session is organised in a coffee shop where the participants watch a video on a specific topic followed by a facilitated discussion.
- A good idea is a medium to accommodate someone's brilliant idea for the company's benefit.
- Retrospect is the vehicle to make tacit knowledge become explicit.
- Cinemania—one gains new knowledge by watching a movie followed by a facilitated discussion.

- A new feature of the K-Club online is the expertise locator, which enables an employee to effectively find an internal expert.

Trainee Journal

- A learning journal for new hires that involves nurturing and coaching from their direct superior.

Planet Learning

- The learning department recently launched a new integrated learning system portal called Planet Learning. Employees can now access required services and information on learning related matters (online course registration, learning events, Mega Mendung learning center, etc.).

Total Productive Maintenance (TPM) System

- TPM is a tool that employees can use as a guide to performing tasks with an institutional basis and to developing a more disciplined culture.
- The primary aim of TPM is to attain "zero accident", "zero breakdown," and "zero defect."
- TPM involves all company departments (production, engineering, quality, development, etc.) within the framework of the eight pillars: autonomous maintenance (AM), planned maintenance (PM), quality maintenance (QM), focused improvement (FI), initial control and maintenance prevention (ICMP), safety, health, and environment (SHE), education and training (E&D) (TPM in the Office).

The Knowledge Club (K-Club) Live

- It offers an interesting way to disseminate knowledge among employees.
- The Knowledge Club online captures organisational knowledge for future utilisation.
- Other programmes are also available, such as SOLAR, Good Idea, Book Club, etc.

Forms of knowledge:

- Explicit knowledge.
- Tacit knowledge.

Methods to Extract Knowledge:

Generative model

- It was the guiding anchor in the process of initiating the "uplifting people engagement" programme.
- The generative coaching model first addressed openness and trust, which are linked with the findings in the above survey.
- The generative coaching model also emphasised the critical link between coaching and the business benefits it brings.
- The four levels of generative coaching allowed for a structured way to integrate coaching in a large organisation like UI over a period of time.

UI wants people to participate passionately in learning activities

- It is a very important initiative for promoting a learning culture in UI and, in time, building a learning organisation.
- UI wants to preserve (tacit) knowledge to fuel future growth.

Knowledge-Sharing

- Sharing information which adds value to an employee in terms of personal development; familiarity with a job process gained from experience.

Skills

- Sharing expertise which directly enhances trainees' ability to perform their jobs well.

Case Study No. 9

Knowledge Management for an IT Company

CITE is an Egyptian IT company having a Professional Services (PS) Division which was suffering loss of organisational memory due to a high turnover rate. In this case study we survey an attempt by the CITE to implement Organisational Memory Information System (OMIS) which supports capturing, gathering and distributing knowledge as Organisational Memory.

OMIS

OMIS was built in CITE starting with the collection of data from internal structure of the PS division by interviewing all employees of the division in order to come up with appropriate factors that need improvement. The Organisational Memory Information System Success Model (OMISSM) was used. The key issues that should be taken into consideration while developing the OMIS were identified. The key factors that affect the development of an efficient OMIS are training, management of OMIS, communication, technology and corporate culture.

Professional Services (PS) and Knowledge Management

Professional Services (PS) form a wide range of activities as systems integration services, legal, accounting and tax consulting services which are all knowledge intensive.

PS firms sell clients their knowledge and its application to specific problems. Therefore, Knowledge Management becomes a critical success factor for success in Professional Services. It is Knowledge Management that enables an organisation the capability to offer clients the benefits of the whole organisation's experience, not just that of a specific project or a specific client's team. This will be made possible only through effective creation, diffusion and use of professional knowledge.

Effectively maintaining PS knowledge is made of many challenges: There exist multiple types of PS knowledge, including market intelligence, best practices, methodologies, topics and tricks – all a part of the discussion around specific assignments and specific engagements. PS knowledge is embedded deep amongst professionals. While such knowledge professionals do engage in knowledge activity as creating, sharing and using knowledge, they operate under certain constraints. For example, they may not manage adequate time for these knowledge management activities and also as their productivity is measured by the billable hours (which do not include the time for these activities). Therefore, they may finally fail to indulge in KM activities.

Role of Technology

Technology, particularly IT has an important role to play in KM implementation in an organisation. Technology can enable KM implementation, enable connections and communications but by itself, cannot make all this happen. It calls for management intervention, as also individuals with interest, commitment for actual happening of all this.

Intranet

Intranet, for example, can empower sharing efforts by integrating databases and information services to provide one stop source for information. Intranet will lower and minimise the communication costs relating to printing, mailing and processing of documents. It can enhance team productivity by creating a collaborative environment, allowing for rapid implementation of KM.

Description of KM Implementation in CS Division of CITE

The PS Division has been providing services to the

local customer base since 1997. They started off with nine consultants focussing mainly on Internet solutions, High Availability (HA) solutions and data management (storage/backup) situations. During the first three years the number of projects meaningfully implemented and delivered was around 70, at an average of seven projects per consultant per year.

By Mid 2000, the company faced a high turnover rate with seven (of nine) leaving the company. The vacancies were replaced and the total number of employees was also increased. However, the revenues fell as the number of successful projects fell. The customer satisfaction level was also decreasing.

Upon interviewing and analysis it was identified that the real reason of this drop was not only turnover rate but the consequences of turnover and its increasing value with elapsed time. The main identifiable problem was the loss of knowledge and its dissipation which affected the revenues drastically. Such knowledge loss had put CITE at great loss and risk in comparison with local market competition. Even though later there were 12 consultants, the reports received from customers showed many negative symptoms as lesser number of projects delivered per year, late implementation of projects, low quality of solutions and poor qualification of the customer's requirements.

The PS Division was relying on Information Systems (IS) to provide all new PS members with the required knowledge and thereby ensure a role being played in organisational memory. But the high turnover rate adversely affected the organisational memory and the company had to find an effective solution for it's IS to better support its organisational memory.

By conducting an internal diagnostics survey it was found by the Management of PS Division that most of the failed projects were implementation projects with multiple vendors integration that were handled by new consultants who lacked the right skills (even though they were expected to have) – for the company's own products – to do their job at the right level, especially when they have all been given extensive training on the company's products. In addition, they were provided with the necessary IS tools to perform at the right level. The main tools provided are based on technologies such as access to Internet, access to PS portal services, access to PS intranet and e-mail. The Management of PS was relying on IS to provide all new PS team members with the requisite knowledge and to play its role in supporting organisational memory. From a KM stand point, these IS tools were built to deal with the company's organisational memory. However, the high turnover rate has resulted in loss of knowledge and has thereby seriously affected the knowledge base of the company, while the IS of the company failed to reach out fully and could not play its expected role in minimising the leakage of knowledge.

Also there are multiple types of knowledge of PS such as best practices, methodologies, tips and tricks and discussions on specific engagements. Therefore, the structure of PS knowledge initiative must accommodate these multiple types. We shall examine the success of CITE in accommodating these multiple types in Knowledge Management initiatives as a Case.

Organisational Memory (OM) of CITE

While there are many definitions for OM, the knowledge of individual workers also is considered as part of OM. OM is defined (by Stein and Zwan) as "the means by which organisational knowledge gets transferred from the past to the present". Often OM is viewed and understood as the persistence of knowledge in the organisation, notwithstanding on how this may be achieved. Such memory may be based on database, files and data. OMIS is viewed as related or based on OM in database, etc. But this may be only partial OM as the entire OM cannot be carried explicit knowledge in database, etc. The tacit component of knowledge will continue to be there in the memories of individual employees. Whatever be the source, the final objective of OM is to improve the competitiveness of the organisation by improving the way in which it manages its knowledge. The knowledge assets and also the learning capacity of a learning organisation can be considered as main source of its competitive advantage.

OMIS Success Model

The OMIS Success Model developed by Jenness, et. al. provides a methodology for measurement of effectiveness of OMIS. If the system in consideration increases organisational effectiveness then it would be considered as OMIS given that it provides a means for bringing past knowledge to bear on present activities. The OMIS Success Model is shown below:

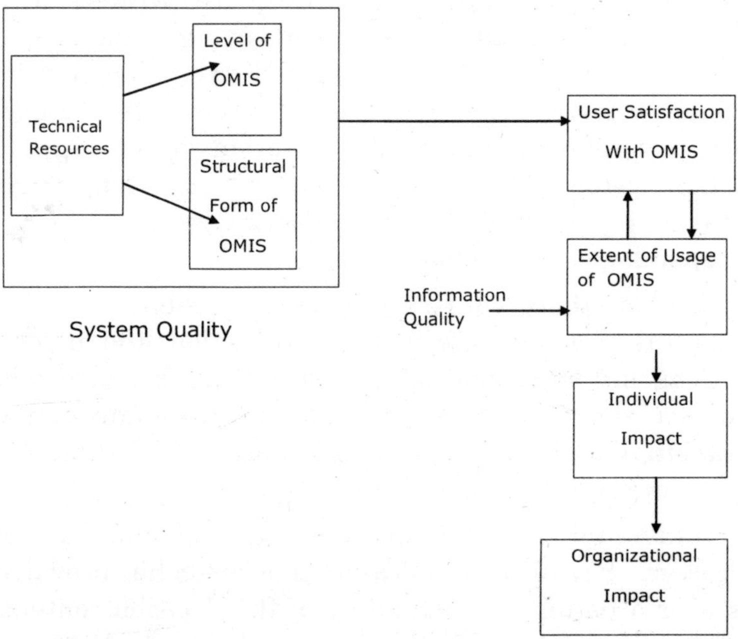

Source: Jenness, *et. al.* (1998).

System Quality, as shown above, describes how good the system is in terms of its operational characteristics.

In this block, Technical Resources describes the capability of the organisation to develop and maintain an OMIS, including aspects such as past experience, technical expertise available to develop and maintain OMIS, the type of hardware used and the competence of users. Evidently this technical expertise impacts both the level of OMIS and the structural form of OMIS (i.e., the extent to which the system is computerised and integrated).

The Form of OMIS also impacts the level of OMIS. Given the effectiveness of IT to provide timely information it is normally presumed that a fully computerised and integrated system will be providing better capability to retrieve past information.

Information Quality defines how good and of what quality is the system in terms of its output. Factors such as importance, relevance, usefulness and informativeness to clarity, content, accuracy and completeness are to be considered in this category. Evidently information quality affects the system usage. System Usage refers to the utilisation of the outputs of the system. User satisfaction is a construct that measures perceptions of the system by users (even independent of its effectiveness).

Both of these constructs provide feedback to each other. Its use will affect user satisfaction and it will, in turn, influence the use. A more satisfied user will increase the usage. As a whole this will impact the individual and such individual impactwill ultimately cause organisational impact.

Individual Impact is produced by individual use of a system. It is also an indication that an IS has provided its user a better understanding of the decision content, has improved the user's decision making, productivity, has produced a change in user activity or has changed decision making perception of the importance of usefulness of IS.

Evidently each individual's impact will have an effect on organisational performance. However, qualitatively the organisational impact may not be simply the summation of individual impacts–it is a complex and difficult relationship.

Challenges in CITE

The data collected has been qualitative (not quantitative) through a questionnaire based on structural interviews, face to face, with all the employees of the company, which include 12 PS consultants and two employees in IS support team. They were made well aware of OMIS before interviews. The main assumption was that the slowdown in IT sector and increased insecurity in IT jobs have not negatively impacted the employees' use of OMIS in terms of knowledge sharing.

The questionnaire mainly focussed on the existing set up of how it supports OMIS, what are the issues that hinder OMIS implementation and what are main areas that need improvement.

These questions resulted in answers which were inputs for OMIS Success Model which had finally led to a realisable framework towards implementation of a successful OMIS. However, it is assumed that all employees have given answers with full integrity and honesty, without any intentional bias, motive or vested interest.

The main limitations of this case study are that the computer documents used in OMIS are e-mail, Intranet and portal services. Paper documents and self (personal) memories are not covered. Also other means of Knowledge Transfer (KT) as direct personal contacts are not covered. Also cultural issues related to KM and OM were also not considered.

Training, Management of OMIS and Communication Limitations

Training is very important for the success of OMIS. Such effective training which resulted in successful Knowledge Transfer was never managed successfully. The new staff has relied on themselves in developing the necessary skills and knowledge on how to effectively use OMIS.

Management of OMIS is very crucial but it does not have a single owner of this task. OMIS comprises several applications and each one of these applications has an owner. Also content is not centrally managed and this may lead to inconsistency problems. Some areas of OMIS may also lack adequate content. CITE did not determine finally what exactly should be made available in the knowledge base nor its location and how it is to be acquired.

There was lack of adequate communication between the owners of different web sites from one side and PS consultants delivering services to customers in the field on the other side. The incomplete and poor content in areas such as integration services has a negative effect on the overall performance of the PS organisation.

Technology has also an important role in success of OMIS. Search engine used in CITE was very basic, lacking high level granularity.

Culture of KM

The corporate culture of CITE encourages the staff to use OMIS, but it is not delivering incentives or acknowledging personal initiatives of knowledge sharing. In other words, while explicit knowledge is shared as it is published on local Intranet web sites or company portal, there was no defined strategy that enables inter personal sharing of knowledge amongst employees. Therefore, it is essential that a corporate wide culture that encourages and rewards knowledge sharing should be developed.

Recommendations

Finally several recommendations were made to CITE management as:

(i) Create a Chief Knowledge Officer position.

(ii) Develop specialised Training Programmes on OMIS.

(iii) Shift corporate culture towards OMIS.

(iv) Develop communication mechanism between PS consultants and content owners, and

(v) Enhance OMIS technical resources.

Conclusion

In this Case Study we have presented the CITE company's problems arising out of lack of effective Knowledge Management. We also indicated solutions in terms of OMIS (Organisational Memory Information System), its success being determined by specific recommendations so that the company can overcome its problems of Knowledge Management.

Case Study No. 10

Knowledge Management in Project Management in Taylor and Woodrow

Taylor and Woodrow is an international construction company based out of the United Kingdom. Its frontline operations are characterised by project management carrying substantial risk. In this Case Study we shall survey how Knowledge Management at Taylor and Woodrow helped reduce the risk by minimising the probability of mischance by promoting best practices and lessons learnt. This Case Study shows how best practices can be developed through knowledge sharing facilitated by network of relationships, both external (between Company and its partners, suppliers and customers) and internal (between frontline managers and construction sites and staff at headquarters). We shall present how knowledge was collated and distributed for mutual benefit of all stake holders, both internal and external.

Background

The Company is an international housing and construction company employing over 7000 people worldwide. Its primary business activity (95 per cent) is house building. This is the second largest house building company in UK, delivering every year about 10000 new homes in UK and about 4000 new homes in other parts of the world as North America, Spain and Gibraltar with different brand names as Bryant Homes in UK, Monarch Homes in Canada and in the rest of the countries as US and Spain with its own name Taylor and Woodrow.

In UK the company operates with a network of 11 regional offices with a central office at West Midlands and construction headquarters at Watford. In addition to housing and commercial property development, the company also undertakes Private Finance Initiative (PFI) projects in UK Govt. health care activity. The company also undertakes facility management and specialised engineering consultancy.

Most (71 per cent) of the revenue comes from UK and the rest from North America (25 per cent) and Spain and Gibraltar (4 per cent). The vision of the company (see http://www.taylorwoodrow.com) is to be "the leading developer of living and working environments in the UK and other chosen markets". The company web site provides full information on the company's stated culture, principles, objectives, responsibility to shareholders, customers and society, business integrity, health, safety and environment, community, competition and corporate governance and other details.

Knowledge Management in the Company

Knowledge Management in the company has been taken care of since 2000 by a central team located at Technology Centre in Leighton Buzzard in UK. The objective is to manage knowledge on a group wide basis. Knowledge Management was initiated by top management as a systematic process to better manage its substantial technical knowledge base. Improving the dissemination of best practices, lessons learned was found to be essential for reducing the technical risks on the projects in addition to reducing the costs of project creation so as to demonstrate added value and business cost differential to the clients. This exercise indeed produced beneficial results so as to reduce the costs to both existing and new clients, thereby help improve the business relationship with the clients. Thus, 2001 onwards Knowledge Management has been integrated into the actual construction project processes to add value which was beneficial to both customers and shareholders.

Description

According to the Company, KM is "primarily about people and how they behave and how they solve problems". The KM process incorporates managers to reduce risks early in the construction process and consider outcomes of actions which were taken in previous projects. This involves management levels of middle and senior managers who actually influence or take all decisions. The Board itself was demonstrating commitment with enthusiasm to implement KM right from the top for the obvious benefits involved. This commitment is a crucial factor for success for any KM initiative in any organisation.

Forum under Knowledge Sharing

A number of knowledge sharing forums were created for different categories as Design Managers, Project Managers and Commercial Managers with an objective to improving processes by sharing knowledge. Each forum was headed by a Senior Manager who was actually seen to be participating, encouraging and ensuring improvements in the practices adopted by participating practitioners through the forum.

While the forum was a platform for sharing knowledge about the best practices, it can also be utilised as a forum for analysing failures or mistakes so as to identify what went wrong and therefore how to prevent it in future. A "Top Tips" bulletin was initiated to be published without the details of identity being provided. Similarly, "Movement for Innovation" was initiated by the Government through which best practices in innovation in projects were captured and disseminated across the entire construction industry.

IT Enabled KM Infrastructure for Knowledge Sharing

The Company's KM manager was the facilitator within the Company who developed and implemented IT enabled KM infrastructure called "Tay Web" for effective distribution of organisational knowledge with the following seven main areas, each of which is a portal in itself:

(a) Company Information – One Company.

(b) News.

(c) People – HR and Training.

(d) The way-we-work – Processes.

(e) Knowledge Share

(f) Central Services

(g) Office Zone – Information on regional office

The knowledge transfer model with eight steps of creating, identifying, collecting and organising best practices and internal knowledge, so as to understand what an organisational part knows and where the knowledge exists.

The process must explicitly address sharing and understanding those practices by motivated recipients. Finally the process involves helping the recipient adopt and apply those practices to new situations to create new "knowledge" to put it into action.

"Tay Web" is Company's intranet which is an entry point to any of the seven portals described above.

"Technical Service News" is an electronic interactive publication summarising the latest technical innovations, legislation and best practices and is available in the knowledge share portal on Tay Web. This provides the Company's in-house technical helpline to online building standards, construction information, online health and safety standards and also provides external web site links for weather and also industry best practice examples. It is also e-mailed on monthly basis to technical staff.

The "Technical Help Desk" (THD) is a facility through which the Company's technology centre offers its specialist technical expertise and help. FAQ (Frequently Asked Questions) lead to Top Tips (technical guidelines) which demonstrates what lessons have been learnt and what innovations have been introduced, both comprising organisational knowledge. The queries to THD will also generate seminars, workshops and training programmes.

During tendering process a significant activity involved is risk assessment and the KM systems provide a vital source of both technical and historical data that project manager's need to access to discover what has been done in the past and what are current best practices. Site engineers also have online access to these guidelines through laptops onsite accessing Internet. If some field personnel need information they can make phone contacts also.

The above can be project specific and can vary from project to project.

Tayweb's Knowledge Share portal comprises a centralised interactive facility available to the entire work force of the company providing a range of library information services. There are also online services such as British Standards, health and safety information, construction information, etc., in addition to access to central technical library and other documents.

Returns from KM initiatives

The main benefits are in terms of use of best practice and lessons learnt to improve quality and reduce defects in the products of the company. Such defects could be causing loss of significant scale in construction industry. Thus, KM supports Quality Management in the Company. Qualitative estimates on Return of Investment (RoI) are also being made.

Conclusion

Taylor Woodrow, the construction company has implemented significant KM initiatives for their benefits in productivity, efficiency and quality management. Substantial returns on investment (RoI) were found to be derived by the Company. In addition, the Company could ensure continuous learning and update for its employees and has also projected itself to its clients as a learning organisation.

Index

D